Additional Praise for *Executive Values*

"'Do unto others as you would have them do unto you'—a simple statement of values recommended by the author to the business leaders of today. If this could have been the prevailing attitude in employer-employee relationships in the recent past . . . what a difference! A valuable and timely message for anyone who has the responsibility of managing people."
—Paul D. Schrage, sr. ex. VP McDonald's Corp. (Retired)

"This important book will move you into a different level of thinking—one of a spiritual perspective and feeling—so necessary in future leadership."
—Richard J. Leider, founding principal, The Inventure Group and author, *Repacking Your Bags*

"Dr. Senske has written a very inspiring, thought-provoking book on organizational leadership. His notes indicate a serious and complete study of considerable background information on a much-needed subject for modern society. I found his treatment of the elements required for a 'balanced' life to be particularly rewarding."
—Merle L. Borchelt, energy consultant and former CEO, Central & South West Corporation (now American Electric Power)

"*Executive Values* is a great mix of insights drawn from management literature, concrete examples garnered from a mix of industries, and Senske's own rich experience seen through the lens of his faith. When leaders root their human relationships and business decisions in enduring faith values, their work is more effective and their lives are more congruent."
—Jill Schumann, president and CEO, Lutheran Services in America

"Kurt Senske reminds us that, for organizational leaders, ethical values must be the bottom line. . . . Dr. Senske shows that living out the golden rule at the personal and organizational level is not only the right thing to do, but it can also provide a steady and powerful course through the turbulent waters of change. All who seek God's guidance in applying Christian faith to daily workplace decisions will find a nutritious meal of food-for-thought in this book."

—Kathryn Wolford, president, Lutheran World Relief

"Executive Values is a strong testimony to Kurt Senske's style of positive, servant leadership ministry that focuses on faith in the Lord and the gifts that God has given his people. . . . *Executive Values* stands for Easter Victory; Energy and Vigor; and Enlightened Vision. It is a valuable new resource for executives and others 'doing well by doing good.'"

—Dr. Richard W. Bimler, speaker, author, and president of Wheat Ridge Ministries

"Here you find critical management principles made even stronger by the application of Christian values in the workplace presented by an author who practices this powerful mix every day in his own successful enterprise. This book is not just a must for managers but should be read by church leaders, pastors, and teachers who minister to and counsel members of their congregations who live in the world of business."

—Roger G. Wheeler, lead director and vice-chairman, Thrivent Financial for Lutherans, a Fortune 300 company

executive

values

A Christian Approach
to Organizational Leadership

Kurt Senske

Augsburg Books
MINNEAPOLIS

For Laurie and Sydney

EXECUTIVE VALUES
A Christian Approach to Organizational Leadership
FIRST PAPERBACK EDITION 2004

Large-quantity purchases or custom editions of this book are available at a discount from the publisher. For more information, contact the sales department at Augsburg Fortress, Publishers, 1-800-328-4648, or write to: Sales Director, Augsburg Fortress, Publishers, P.O. Box 1209, Minneapolis, MN 55440-1209.

The full text of the Johnson & Johnson Credo (in several languages) and a history of its development can be seen at the company Web site (www.jnj.com). © Johnson & Johnson. Used by permission.

"Growing the Next Generation: Mentoring is a tool for cultivating new leaders," *Life@Work Journal*, September, 1998, p. 18, 20.

"Balance Life's Juggling Act," by Dr. Stephen Graves and Thomas Addington, *Life@Work Journal*, November/December 2000, pp. 40, 43.

Eight step program to produce meaningful, lasting change, from *Leading Change* by John Kotter. (Cambridge: Harvard Business School Press, 1996), pp. 3-16

Scripture passages are from the Holy Bible, New International Version, copyright © 1973, 1978, 1984 International Bible Society. Used by permission of Zondervan Publishing House. All rights reserved.

ISBN 0-8066-5153-9 (paperback)

Cover design by Sarah Gioe; front cover photo © Premium Stock/CORBIS
Book design by Michelle L. N. Cook

The Library of Congress has cataloged the hardcover edition as follows
Senske, Kurt Martin, 1959-
 Executive values : a Christian approach to organizational leadership /
by Kurt Senske.
  p. cm.
Includes bibliographical references (p.).
 ISBN 0-8066-4554-7
 1. Executives—Religious life. 2. Management—Religious aspects—Christianity. I. Title.

BV4596.E93 S46 2003
248.8'8—dc21   2002153752

Manufactured in Canada

08   07   06   05   04   1   2   3   4   5   6   7   8   9   10

contents

acknowledgments

Executive Values **has truly been a** team effort. In a perfect world, everyone who is mentioned below would be listed on the jacket cover. First and foremost, this book simply would not have been written if not for the early encouragement of my wife, Laurie. She believed in this project and my ability to see it through to completion long before I did, and kept encouraging me to "get back at it" even though it meant even less time together as a family. Laurie and I, along with our seven-year-old daughter, Sydney, are truly a team in every sense of the word, together striving to add value in this world through our everyday actions.

Throughout my career I have been blessed to work with some wonderful mentors and colleagues, all of whom have helped shape and develop the leadership framework laid out in *Executive Values*. This list includes Les Bayer, Don Bokenkamp, Pat Bokenkamp, Craig Borchardt, JoAnn Brashear, Bob Greene, Keith Eckelkamp, Jim Hammond, David Kahle, Katherine Kerr, Jack Loftus, John Long, Bruce Nicholson, DJ Sartorio, Sam Sipes, Bill Thompson, David Yarborough, and the talented and dedicated staff of Lutheran Social Services of the South. You have taught me how to be a leader and for that I am grateful.

I also owe a debt of gratitude to the following successful Christ-based leaders who took time out of their busy schedules to dialogue with me about the topic of this book. I especially want to thank Don Bokenkamp, Merle Borchelt, U.S. House Majority Leader Tom DeLay, Bobby Griffin, Brad Hewitt, Jim Hushagen, Richard Kessler, Ed Kruse, Richard Leider, John Mackovic, Earl Maxwell, John McDaniels, Bruce Nicholson, Jill Schumann, Albert Siu, Dick Tesauro, and Lynn Walker. Their values-based leadership philosophy and insights have influenced my approach to leadership and are incorporated in this book.

Steve Wenk critiqued an early draft of this manuscript. Without his help this book would have remained unpublished. My parents, Al and Ruth Senske, also deserve heartfelt thanks for their valuable feedback and support. Karen Ashorn deserves special mention for her diligent proofreading and skill at keeping my calendar clear on occasion to allow me to finish this book. I also appreciate the sabbatical that the Board of Directors of Lutheran Social Services of the South provided me to finish this book. Their servant-leadership approach to governance has added lasting value to our organization.

Michael Wilt is not only a gifted editor at Augsburg Fortress, he has also become a friend. He was invaluable at bringing *Executive Values* to fruition. For someone who is not versed in the nuances of organizational leadership, he has an uncanny knack for seeing the big picture and providing me with language and structure that bring life to my ideas on paper.

And finally, I thank you for trusting me enough to take seriously my Christ-based framework of leadership. My hope and prayer is that, together, we can continue to make a difference in this world through our organizational lives. I look forward to continuing this journey with you today and, God willing, for years to come.

preface

We make a living by what we get, but we make a life by what we give.
—Winston Churchill

Two events that took place during the writing of this book have had a profound impact on our organizational and personal lives. The first, of course, was the series of terrorist attacks on September 11, 2001. Like most people who witnessed the tragic events of that day from afar, I was initially overwhelmed with the need to be with the people who are truly the most important to me—in my case my wife and daughter. I was also overwhelmed with a feeling of helplessness and insignificance. I felt called upon to make a difference and help the victims and their families, and I had no idea how to do so. The good that I was accomplishing in my professional career seemed suddenly inadequate in the context of September 11.

Although not nearly as catastrophic, the second event that captured our collective attention during the writing of this book was the Enron fiasco. We witnessed with disbelief the destruction of some $70 billion in wealth that decimated the retirement savings of thousands of Enron employees and punished even more small investors. We were enraged and dismayed as congressional hearings demonstrated proof of an intentional strategy by senior management to misrepresent financial transactions for the purpose of enriching themselves at the expense of those they were entrusted to serve. We felt abandoned by two supposedly premier organizations, Enron and Arthur Andersen, and wondered just whom we could ever trust again. We later discovered that other supposedly premier organizations—Adelphia, Dynergy, Global Crossing, Merrill Lynch, Qwest, Tyco, and WorldCom, to name just a few—had also engaged in greed-driven and unethical activity that enriched those at the top at the expense of employees, customers, and shareholders. Our willingness to trust in such organizations, and the markets in which they operate, was further challenged.

So much destruction and deceit are bound to cause society and individuals to engage in intensive self- and collective examination and reflection. In the months that followed these two events, two important elements of personal and organizational life that had been buried during the economic boom of the 1990s began to slowly resurface. First, many of us came to the realization that we have for too long compartmentalized our lives into work, home, and church, and have applied different standards to each. We have come to see that values, ethics, and spirituality—however one chooses to describe them—cannot be checked at the office door. The standards we live by at home, in church, and among family and friends should be incorporated in the workplace. People at all levels of an organization, from the boardroom to the factory floor, are searching to connect their faith and values to their professional lives in a way that brings both personal fulfillment and organizational success.

Second, for-profit and nonprofit organizations alike are reawakening to the age-old idea that values and organizational success are in fact inseparable. In what Alan Greenspan describes as "capitalized reputation," our society is in the midst of creating a new trust-based economy where an organization's value and success is inextricably linked to its reputation.

Numerous post-September 11 and post-Enron conversations with those in the suites, as well as those in the cubicles, revealed that people intuitively understand that values and long-term success are inseparable. What is lacking, however, is a framework or blueprint that provides guidance for taking our "whole selves" to work. Christians, too, often lack the framework and language that will help them put their faith-based principles into practice in the workplace. Despite their good intentions, a myriad of workplace pressures and daily obstacles prevent them from achieving this goal.

Executive Values is a first step in educating Christian organizational leaders on how to incorporate systematically their values into their professional lives. If the golden rule, "Do unto others as you would have them do unto you," had been followed at the highest levels of Enron, Arthur Andersen, and the myriad of other corporations that recently have come under fire for questionable practices, we as a society may have avoided the damaging aftereffects of scandals and congressional inquiries. By following the golden rule at work as well as at home, we can add value to our organization and those around us. We can bring our "whole selves" to work and make a life instead of merely making a living.

Kurt Senske
Austin, Texas
Spring 2003

introduction

do well
by doing good

There is no reason you can't be one of the most successful organizations in the world and one of the most altruistic. There is no inconsistency between those goals.
—Jim Collins

This book combines two aspects of organizational leadership not often mentioned in the same breath: getting results and integrating Christian values within an organization. Leaders of organizations recognize that results matter. Results, in fact, are the sole reason any organization exists, whether in the public or private sector, whether with nonprofit or for-profit status. Yet it seems that modern business practice dictates that organization leaders, in order to achieve profitable results, must keep their professional lives and their lives as faithful Christians separate. *Executive Values* serves as a road map for incorporating faith and values into everyday organizational life. It demonstrates how doing *well* and doing *good* are inextricably linked, and provides a comprehensive strategy for utilizing Christian values to achieve organizational goals.

Results are measured in various ways, depending on the type of organization involved. In a school environment, educational outcomes may be primary; while in a publicly traded company, maximizing shareholder return is foremost. Complicating this is the fact that many organizations have goals that seem contradictory. For example, a hospital exists to provide excellent care for the customer, but its leadership is also responsible for maximizing shareholder return. The pressure created by having multiple goals can lead to confused priorities and seem to force a decision between altruism and financial reality. This in turn makes it difficult for business leaders to consistently apply Christ-centered values as they navigate the minefields of daily organizational life. The "mines" are familiar: budgetary pressures, shortsighted investors, unrealistic sales goals, difficult employee issues, new competitors, and disloyal customers. This book is for the organization leader who is a Christian and who seeks to achieve an organization's stated goals while struggling daily to live out the ideals formed through faith. It is my belief that God does not ask us to have a successful career at the expense of our faith. At work, at home, and at play, I believe that God desires that we strive to pattern our lives after the life and teachings of Christ. Further, I believe that incorporating Christian faith-based values into our daily professional life gives us a competitive advantage. Consistently doing so can have a significant positive impact on your organization and on your personal life.

Executive Values is a "how-to" book designed to help you succeed in your chosen profession without compromising your faith and losing your soul in the process. Jesus warns against seeking worldly recognition and power at the expense of faith: "What good will it be for a man if he gains the whole world, yet forfeits his soul?" (Matt. 16:26). As every organization leader knows all too well, the temptations to "gain the whole world" are numerous. How often has a boss asked an employee to fudge financial data, or to front-date sales invoices in order to meet certain quotas? Or what director of a nursing home has not felt pressure to reduce the number of direct-care staff or downgrade the quality of food in order to meet budgetary goals? While such strategies may work in the short run, in the long term they are always detrimental.

History is replete with examples of shortsighted and less-than-ethical bosses whose companies prosper in the present but eventually receive their due. The lure of work can also have damaging effects on one's personal life: the executive who spends too many hours at the office may one day discover that her zealousness has drained her of creativity and destroyed her marriage. Just as harmful are piecemeal decisions made by well-intentioned leaders in a vacuum, divorced from any overarching strategic plan and decision-making framework that can also negatively impact an organization, its customers, and its employees.

Difficult philosophical questions are nothing new to businesses and their leaders. If anything, they seem to have become more challenging as the world has grown more complex. Is it morally justifiable to shut down an inefficient manufacturing plant, resulting in great pain and financial hardship for employees, their families, and their community? Is it ethical to fire a twenty-year employee who is no longer getting the job done? Is it okay for a college president to close an underutilized academic department, thereby putting at peril the future of a dozen tenured and dedicated faculty members? Just what *is* the right thing to do? I propose that these need not be either/or decisions. It is my contention that the Christian leader has a responsibility to develop and implement a framework in which both doing *well* and doing *good* are attainable. I hope to demonstrate how difficult decisions, which on the surface may appear callous, can be made for the right reasons and implemented in a compassionate manner. I hope to show how adhering to Christian values in dealing with employees and customers is always good for business. This book is based on the belief that leaders need not "check" Christian values at the corporate door in order to succeed professionally, and that these values—values formed at home, through Bible study, and at church—are the very building blocks of success and excellence.

Many business leaders stumble over the reality that values and achievement go hand in hand. Leaders too often feel "caught" in having to make the Hobson's choice between what is best for their organization and what is right in terms of upholding their Christian values. Laura Nash, in her book *Believers in Business*,[1] lists what she believes to be seven tensions Christians experience in business:

1. serving God versus pursuing profit
2. love versus competition
3. people needs versus profit obligations
4. family versus work
5. keeping personal perspective in the face of success
6. charity versus wealth
7. being a faithful witness in a pluralistic workplace

While Nash has captured well the choices presented to many Christian leaders, my professional experience has taught me that these choices are not mutually exclusive. Playing out our professional, religious, and personal lives is not a zero-sum game. Taken individually, it may indeed be that each tension Nash proposes presents us with a difficult choice. I argue, however, that when these "choices" are viewed in their totality against the backdrop of faith, the tension disappears. Then we can see how our Christian underpinnings work together with our God-given talents to succeed as organization leaders. For too long we have remained stuck, feeling we must choose between attaining business success on the one hand, and living out our Christian principles on the other.

What I propose, then, is a way that allows business leaders to use their Christian values to succeed both professionally and personally; that enables leaders to combine the love of competition with the desire to work toward the betterment of humankind; and that enables leaders to give due attention to both family and career. I believe God intends for us to live our lives to the fullest at home and at work, to maximize our capabilities to achieve God's will, and to make the world a better place. In fact, in order to achieve true success and happiness in life, there is no other way.

On the surface, the guidelines I offer to leaders who are Christian seem fairly simple and straightforward:

- develop a close relationship with God
- strive for professional success
- have a close relationship with family
- adhere to Christian values in dealing with others
- achieve organizational goals
- provide good leadership
- make a difference in people's lives
- share Christ with others

Many good self-help business books on the market address principles and guidelines such as these. Among them are *Seven Habits of Highly Effective People* by Stephen Covey; *The Power Principle: Influence with Honor* by Blaine Lee; *Halftime: Changing Your Game Plan from Success to Significance* by Bob Buford; *The Power of Purpose: Creating Meaning in Your Life and Work* by Richard Leider; and *Leadership from the Inside Out* by Kevin Cashman. These books propose helpful theoretical models for effective leadership. What they do not provide are concrete ideas and suggestions on how to handle common situations in the workplace that daily test our Christian framework of values. In fact, Buford, in his otherwise valuable book, seems to suggest—wrongly, I believe—that having to make decisions that conflict with Christian values is an unfortunate but probably inevitable fact of life at the beginning stages of a career (in his case, determining whether his television empire should air a pornography channel).

Executive Values goes beyond theory to practical, everyday advice and insight for implementing faith in effective leadership. It demonstrates, among other things, how Christian values provide a basis for attracting and retaining good employees; creating a Christ-based, effective organizational culture; implementing a successful vision and strategic plan; and successfully balancing career and family life. It also proposes a framework for making decisions in specific situations—like whether to lay off five, fifty, or even five hundred employees in order to increase shareholder value, or how to deal with an ineffective employee whose spouse is ailing with cancer. Do I accept the job offer from another company, and the $50,000 pay increase that comes with it, or do I stay in my present position, where I have been for less than a year? Where do I find the courage to make tough decisions now, when the company is doing well, even though I know that the picture will not be so rosy in the years ahead? How do I choose between going on vacation with my family and handling the emergency that came up at work? In the case of multibillion-dollar companies, decisions made—and their repercussions—can be extremely far-reaching. Leaders face such situations every day. Nike's decision to offer region-specific market wages in developing countries had ethical implications and marketplace consequences. Exxon, in its offshore drilling operations, had to decide what level of pollution was "acceptable" when balanced against global environmental concerns. Firestone and Ford were forced to grapple with the safety level of their products, and with notifying the public about such concerns in a timely manner. All of the leadership decisions related to these issues had global implications.

The framework I propose on the following pages has been developed over the past eighteen years and is drawn from my experience as president and CEO of a $70 million-dollar organization with more than twelve hundred employees; as an attorney with various Chicago law firms; as a political consultant at the local, state, and national levels; as a college administrator; and as a member of the boards of a Fortune 300 company, a national, religious nonprofit organization, and a national foundation. More importantly, I have relied heavily on what other Christians have taught me about leadership. These are individuals who, for decades, have put their values into action. They are from all walks of life, including small-business leaders, organizational consultants, colleagues, CEOs of Fortune 500 companies, heads of nonprofit organizations, the football coach at a major university, and a U.S. congressional leader. In addition, I have interviewed leaders in both the public and private sectors, taking the "best from the best."

The fundamental purpose of *Executive Values* is to provide a blueprint for decision making that reflects Christian values in the carrying out of day-to-day responsibilities both at work and at home. The following chapters are divided along the lines of function. I propose a theoretical framework for Christian leadership and examine the experiences of successful leaders. I also present real-life examples of the challenges faced by leaders, along with potential solutions. The book also provides practical guidelines for applying Christian values in typical leadership situations, such as implementing a strategic planning process, creating a healthy organizational culture, developing future leaders, holding people accountable, and balancing work and family life.

The topic of this book is vital and relevant. It is through our professional lives that we have the greatest opportunity to make a difference in the world. During our lifetime, each of us will spend from eighty thousand to one hundred thousand of our most productive hours at work, influencing the lives of thousands. And while most of us are diligent about living out our Christian principles at church, at home, and through our volunteer efforts, we are not always as successful doing so at work. This is a book that will help leaders apply the Christian values—nurtured by family, colleagues, and church—to achieve their professional dreams and to attain goals laid out for oneself and the organization. In essence, it will demonstrate that you can, in fact, do well by doing good. My hope is that *Executive Values* will be of value to you, and an asset to the business community at large.

chapter one

follow the golden rule of leadership

The leader for today and the future will be focused on how to be—how to develop quality, character, mind-set, values, principles, and courage.

—Francis Hesselbein

A multitude of books has been written on leadership. Teaching someone how to be a leader, however, is an impossible task. Most, if not all, of the characteristics of an effective leader come from within. That does not mean that the subject of leadership should be ignored; rather, in order to improve our leadership skills, it is vital that we explore our own "within."

Having a high-powered job, or the title of president, director, or manager, does not make one a leader. Neither is effective leadership the result of charisma, physical prowess, education, or experience. All of these qualities can be useful in specific situations, but they do not make a leader. Peter Drucker says, "The only definition of a *leader* is someone who has *followers*."[1] We must ask ourselves the question: How do we acquire followers? The answer for us as Christians begins with the understanding that true leadership comes through one's own Christian values and authenticity combined with a deep desire to create value through achieving the mission of your organization.

The Golden Rule

As children, we were taught the golden rule: "So in everything, do to others, what you would have them do to you . . ." (Matt. 7:12). This is not merely the latest in a long series of trendy management techniques. It is a sound business principle that has been around since at least the time of Christ, and continues to be taught by the top business schools in the land. Brad Hewitt, former CEO and president of Diversified Pharmaceutical Services, describes his time at the Harvard University Business School as a "very expensive lesson in learning that following the golden rule is what makes organizations successful over the long term." Besides learning what he calls a few useful "rocket science" financial models, Hewitt holds that the golden rule is "the primary lesson that I came away with during my time at Harvard."[2]

The Golden Rule of Leadership works because it provides personal growth in employees and sustained economic growth in organizations. It incorporates the gospel values of love, honesty, respect, and justice into our daily decision making and actions. The Golden Rule of Leadership adds lasting value in that it is other-directed, not self-centered; it builds people up as opposed to using them up; it allows people to envision new possibilities rather than seeing themselves and the world as unchangeable; it invites decision making based on one's values; and it allows everyone within the organization to reveal their inner values without forcing others to change their beliefs. As a caveat, the reason we as Christian leaders adhere to the golden rule is not to achieve earthly success. The golden rule should be adhered to because it is what God instructs us to do. What this book demonstrates, however, is that in addition to following God's will, the Golden Rule of Leadership provides us with the underlying principle to also achieve superior organizational results and lead meaningful lives. Following the Golden Rule of Leadership will allow us to shine the light of our faith into the marketplace and possibly even refute the statement by the

Harvard theologian Paul Tillich, who wrote, "Any serious Christian must be a socialist."[3]

Research and experience unequivocally demonstrate that if you are intent on doing what is best for the long-term interests of your organization, it is imperative that you consistently apply the golden rule. It must be carried out as you create your organizational culture, engage in strategic planning, mentor and develop those around you, and maintain a healthy balance between work and personal life. The remainder of this book will demonstrate with data and anecdotes how implementing the Golden Rule of Leadership will provide you with a framework to achieve your organizational and personal goals.

Becoming an authentic leader starts from within. Ken Blanchard, noted author and business consultant, acknowledges that he was frustrated early in his career by the fact that many business leaders talked a good game about implementing the newest management technique or leadership style in their organizations, but quickly reverted back to the "old ways" of doing business when they were in the trenches of day-to-day management. He later realized that this was, at bottom, an issue of character. In order for people to modify their behavior, they must first change from within. And this requires a transformation of the heart.[4]

Each person reading this book is at a different stage of developing the right heart for leadership. We as Christians have an advantage in that we intuitively understand what it means to have a right heart. But this is a lifelong quest. Leadership is a journey, not a destination; it is not brain knowledge, but heart knowledge. It is a 'round-the-clock, conscious effort to lead a professionally and personally God-pleasing life. It is the willingness to develop a framework of leadership that allows the incorporation of values into organizational life in a way that is both systematic and successful. True leadership from within is the result of our deep relationship and constant dialogue with our Lord and Savior. I have found that this relationship is strengthened, and I become empowered, when I keep close to the Scriptures, commit myself to regular Bible study, and surround myself with healthy friends and mentors. There are a number of excellent resources that can help develop the right heart for leadership. I have found Richard Leider's *The Power of Purpose*,[5] along with Kevin Cashman's *Leadership from the Inside Out*,[6] to be especially helpful. Other useful resources include *Jesus on Leadership* by C. Gene Wilkes[7] and *Leadership by the Book* by Ken Blanchard et al.[8]

Christians who are on the path of becoming authentic leaders who desire to create value in an organization and in private life are naturally intent on applying Christian principles to these activities. Many have implemented these principles on a piecemeal basis. What is needed, however, is a comprehensive framework to apply Christian values in a way that allows leaders to be authentic and to create real value for an organization over the long term.

The Characteristics of a Christ-based Leader

Being a Christian leader means living under God's guidance and according to Christian principles, and always asking the question, "Am I building people up, or am I building myself up and merely using those around me?" Under Christ-based leadership, people are not the means to an end; rather, they *are* the end. People matter. For the leader who truly values them, others become partners in achieving shared organizational goals. What are the characteristics of a Christ-based leader?

Christ-based leaders are servant leaders

A Christ-based leader is first and foremost a "servant leader." Understanding the idea of servant leadership begins with Jesus, who described the idea in this manner: "Whoever wants to be great among you must be your servant, and whoever wants to be first among you must be your slave, just as the Son of Man did not come to be saved, but to serve, and to give his life as a ransom for many" (Matt. 20:26-28).

Any Christian leader who wishes to incorporate this understanding into a leadership framework must begin by solidifying his or her own relationship with God. No one can become a servant leader without first submitting to God, or in other words, subordinating one's rights and desires to the service of God and others. As words on a page, this might appear to be simple and obvious, but on an immediate, practical level, the choice to submit to God has serious ramifications. It might, for example, mean giving credit to others when it is due them; it might even mean directing others to take over the leadership role if they are better suited for the task at hand. It is a challenge that requires daily care and attention.

But the true strength of this perspective is that it gives leaders the freedom to take the lessons of the Gospel and apply them to the everyday tasks of leadership. I make this concept operational by striving, daily, to incorporate the golden rule in all that I do.

In its elegant simplicity, this Christ-given philosophy of servant leadership calls us to tend genuinely to those with whom we interact—customers, colleagues, family, community; to accept as our own the mistakes of others; to create an environment that allows for accountability and responsibility; to take into account the needs of all members of the community; to establish a values system based on biblical principles; and to create an environment that allows others the freedom to live out their deeply held values.

As will be demonstrated throughout this book, being a servant leader by following the golden rule provides us with a biblically based framework to achieve significant results and lead a meaningful, balanced, Christ-centered life. It allows us to love and live as Jesus did. And, in following Christ's footsteps, create through example and invitation other disciples to accomplish God's work in the world.

Without servant leadership, none of the tools incorporated into a particular leadership style will be effective. Blanchard,

Hybels, and Hodges talk about the importance of being a servant leader in our intellect, our emotions, and our behavior—the head, the heart, and the hands.[9] I understand this to mean that, first, true leadership cannot be faked, and, second, that it must encompass our whole being as God has created us. It must be an integral part of our lifestyle and of our core existence at home, at work, and in the community. Excellent resources that help define servant leadership include Robert Greenleaf's *Servant Leadership*;[10] Laurie Beth Jones's *Jesus, CEO*[11] Max DePree's *Leadership Is an Art*[12] as well as *Leadership Jazz*;[13] and James C. Hunter's *The Servant.*[14]

But leadership it is not a one-person show. Servant leadership will have an impact on an organization only if those around the leader embrace it as well. For this to happen, a leader must be the role model. For example, if it is important to you as a leader that your staff not work late hours, you must model this behavior. Bobby Griffin, former executive vice president of Medtronic, describes how Bill George, Medtronic's CEO, would go home by 5:00 P.M. on the days he was not traveling, in order to be with his family. Everyone knew not to disturb him until after 8:30 P.M., when he would retire to his home office to take phone calls and finish his day's work.[15] George personally modeled the values that he helped instill in the Medtronic culture.

For every such positive example of servant leadership, there are hundreds of examples of unhealthy and even damaging leadership styles. On a recent plane trip, I sat next to a senior manager of a Fortune 500 company who was returning from a managers' meeting led by the company's senior vice president. After peering over my shoulder and noticing that I was writing a book on management, he shared with me what had taken place at the meeting. The senior vice president had flown in on the company plane (everyone else was asked to go coach) and arrived in a town car at the hotel with his entourage of staff, where he lodged in the hotel suite. The rest of the participants arrived on the hotel shuttle and, naturally, had standard rooms. The next day, this executive gave the managers a "pep talk" on the importance of cutting costs during this temporary period of economic slowdown. Needless to say, he was not well received by the audience. This executive's actions did not coincide with his message. What my flight partner "heard" was that he must cut costs so that this executive could keep up his standard of living. Not a very compelling vision! While the manager was smart enough to pay lip service to the cost-cutting request, it was clear from his behavior that his heart and soul were not in it. It is difficult to respect a boss who fails to serve the organization while demanding significant sacrifices from employees.

Christ-based leaders are leaders you can trust

Trust flows naturally when one leads by serving as a Christ-based servant leader. Still, trust must be earned; it is a reward that accrues over time. It is the result of openness and integrity. Michael Useem, director of the Center for Leadership and Change at the University of Pennsylvania's Wharton School of Business, describes trust as "the accumulated product of saying what you're going to do, and doing it, and getting results."[16] Trust results from being true to the goal of acting with integrity and authenticity, and from keeping promises made to employees, customers, and clients. It also has tangible benefits—the end result is improved loyalty from employees, customers, and suppliers, greater cost advantages through better productivity, and more loyal investors.[17] Trustworthy leadership in nonprofit organizations has the benefit of creating stakeholders who will be more devoted and active, and increased potential for support from funding sources and donors.

A leader's immediate sphere of influence includes his or her "direct reports." The key for success is to work tirelessly to strengthen bonds of trust with direct reports and, by being a good role model, to instill in the organization a culture that encourages direct reports to develop similarly trusting relationships with those who report directly to them. This ripple effect will transform the entire organization.

Trust also has direct benefits for Christian leaders ourselves. First, it gives us the right to have our message heard. Second, doing business becomes more efficient. As Francis Fukuyama notes, "If people who have to work together in an enterprise trust one another because they are all operating according to a common set of ethical norms, doing business costs less."[18] Third, it ensures that our key people will remain loyal to us and to the organization during both bad times and good times. Fourth, it helps create a shared sense of purpose, which will, in turn, empower others to make those routine daily decisions that are key to the organization's operation. Fifth, it empowers our managers to hire employees with similar values. Sixth, it allows us to take a vacation without worrying about what is happening in our absence. And, finally, it assures us that our employees are treating customers in the way that we would treat them.

Trust flows two ways. If we expect complete honesty from our employees, then leaders, too, must be rigorously forthcoming. Part of being a servant-leader is to openly admit our mistakes. In my position as CEO, I make it a point to include, in addressing board meetings, stakeholders, and employees, examples not just of our successes but of times we have not lived up to our standards as well. As a result, I have developed a reputation as a straight shooter, and as a leader who can be trusted. People will forgive our mistakes. They will respect us for sharing with them news they do not want to hear. They will not forgive us for white-washing a problem or for being dishonest.

Christ-based leaders hire people with similar values

Hiring people who possess similar values provides a mechanism to ensure that the principles of servant leadership are adopted throughout the organization. Not only does the leader have to "walk the walk" and "talk the talk," but so do others throughout the organization. The simple reality is that it is not in the organization's best interest to hire or to tolerate an employee who has a harmful managerial style—no matter how talented he or she may be in other respects. Morale will suffer, productivity will decrease, and good employees will vote with their feet. Nearly everyone has a story of such a person in the midst of an organization—an individual who possesses enormous talent, who is a great salesperson, who has all the required skill sets, but who does not know how to get along and work effectively with others. As a result, teamwork becomes impossible, meetings become confrontational, and good people leave the organization.

As Christians, we have a duty to work with these individuals—to help them understand their weaknesses and assist them to grow in their personal and professional lives. I have sent employees to American Management Association courses; used the 360 process, an evaluation tool that allows for honest feedback from all who come in contact with that employee; provided leadership coaches; and spent considerable amounts of time in dialogue with them about the impact of their performance on our organization. Some have responded well. Other times, however, I have had to let employees go because of a negative management style and an inability or unwillingness to change. Letting someone go is always a difficult step, at best. It is, nonetheless, sometimes required. One president of a large manufacturing organization told me about his vice president of sales, a woman who was very talented, but who had a combative management style. For the five years she was with the company, it doubled in size. Because of this success he was afraid to let her go. Looking back, however, the president believes the company would have quadrupled in size had he asked her to leave earlier. Her personality poisoned the organizational culture, which resulted in the company becoming inefficient and less productive.

Because of the advantages of staffing an organization with people of similar values, the question of letting an employee go because of a "bad fit" becomes an ethical issue. Is it the Christian thing to do? My experience has been that in certain situations the answer is a resounding yes. Removing an employee whose presence is harmful is a decision that will ultimately have a favorable influence on the lives of others in the organization. This is in keeping with the first responsibility of a servant leader: to add long-term value to the organization. And, in many cases, letting a person go also does that person a favor. It sometimes takes such a drastic measure for an employee to make the kind of honest self-examination that can improve the quality of his or her life and work. One former top executive in our organization wrote me a three-page letter thanking me for letting him go. He said it "forced" him to reexamine his life, which led to personal counseling to work through issues he had pretended did not exist. He has now started a new career, and is continuing to incorporate into his professional and personal life the changes he has made. This man had found his calling—something that would not have occurred had I not taken the step to let him go. If a leader remains focused on the goal of adding long-term value and truly cares about the individual in question, he or she will make the right decision. As we will discuss in detail in chapter 6, having made our decision, we as Christians have a responsibility to carry it out in a compassionate, Christian manner.

Christ-based leaders pay attention to public relations

Another often-overlooked aspect of the servant-leadership strategy is the supporting role of public relations. Public relations and marketing departments can enhance the impact of servant leadership on achieving an organization's goals. A recent survey by the public relations firm of Burson-Marsteller revealed that 40 percent of a company's reputation is based on how others— investors, donors, suppliers, customers, and the company's employees—perceive the CEO.[19] Al Lauer, CEO of Varian, a technology and measurement systems company, correctly notes that "Shareholders, employees, and customers are three legs of the reputation stool. The CEO must build trust within each group."[20] The criteria for evaluation include the leader's character, skills as a manager, and ability to be a visionary. The reputation of a CEO, says Jeffrey Sonnenfeld, is "part of the branding process we use to simplify complex relationships. CEOs tend to personify the values one associates with the [organization's] reputation."[21] One executive who understands this process is Herb Kelleher, longtime CEO and sitting chairman of Southwest Airlines. His public persona greatly influenced the airline's organizational culture for the good. Similarly, good public relations also means admitting one's mistakes. It means, for example, admitting to stakeholders that customer service currently does not meet our expectations and sharing what we are doing to fix the problem.

Recognizing the power of public relations may seem like common sense, but many leaders pay little attention to this aspect of servant leadership. This neglect is a result, in part, of equating servant leadership with a misguided sense of humility, and ignoring the benefits that a positive public display of organizational values can bring about. While these leaders may be of sterling character, and may truly value their employees, they fail to present these qualities effectively to their internal and external audiences. Let me give you an example. My predecessor as CEO of a large social service agency was a very talented executive. He had spent sixteen years building the agency from a small, failing group to a successful $30 million organization responsible for providing needed services every day to more than six thousand individuals. It became apparent to me, however, that many of our stakeholders—donors, customers, and employees—did not always view him in a favorable light. He was mistakenly perceived as arrogant, aloof, and self-centered. This resulted in stakeholders who believed in our mission but did not always commit personally to adding further value to the organization. The misguided public perception of this good man prevented us from reaching our full potential. For those of us who knew this individual—and I consider him to be one of my mentors—this negative perception could not have been further from the truth. But for better or worse, perception is reality, and our organization suffered as a result.

Upon becoming CEO, I immediately began to develop a plan to change this perception of our organization. I knew it had to start with how our stakeholders viewed me, the new guy. I came in at a time when we were losing more than $1 million a year. In the face of this downward spiral, I added $200,000 to our public relations budget. In addition, I personally visited all of our major stakeholders, and fifty senior managers, with the goal of listening to their concerns and dreams. Our public relations people began placing me before the media, getting op-ed pieces published in local newspapers, and arranging for interviews on radio and television. We also began pursuing celebrity personalities to become involved with our organization. People began to see us relating publicly to highly recognizable people, including then-Texas Governor George W. Bush, U.S. House Majority Leader Tom DeLay, former University of Texas head football coach John Mackovic, television personality Phyllis George, singer Willie Nelson, and local television newscasters. In today's media-focused world, these associations helped give us needed credibility and public exposure. Of course, all our efforts at good public relations would not matter if we failed to deliver consistently a quality product. Good intentions are not enough. Results matter. So at the same time, our leadership team renewed our commitment to systems that would ensure consistent quality care throughout the programs we operated. With all that in mind, we created a culture in which quality care was systematically and objectively measured.

Did our efforts pay off? A year after we began this intentional effort to overhaul our reputation, I received a phone call from a farmer who had also done well in the oil industry, and whom we had unsuccessfully tried to recruit as a major donor. He told me that he heard me being interviewed on the radio when he was driving to town to pick up some supplies. "It sounds like you're doing a good job," he said. "Why don't you come over sometime to visit." That interaction, along with many other such opportunities, led to a growth in our annual donations from $2 million to $5 million. Other things also began to happen: Our surveys indicated that our stakeholders now had a higher opinion of our organization; the state of Texas began asking us to develop programs on their behalf for poor and abused children; Governor Bush and his staff lifted up our organization as a model of success on his presidential campaign Web site, as well as in some of his speeches; and, most importantly, the number of people we served increased from six thousand to eight thousand. This entire initiative worked because of three primary factors: As the person in the organization with the highest profile, my personal and public behavior matched the persona our public relations department highlighted in our campaign; our senior management team shared similar values; and we provided top-quality services. Through all of this, I learned that one's reputation as a servant-leader matters. While it must be cultivated in our heart, it must also be visible in our actions and in our public-relations strategy.

Christ-based leaders make everyone a leader

Another aspect that is critical to effective leadership is the importance of making everyone in the organization a leader. Jack Welch, long-time CEO of General Electric, observed that it is usually the person doing the actual work who knows the right answer. He commented that it was "embarrassing to reflect that for probably eighty or ninety years, we've been dictating equipment needs and managing people who know how to do things much better and faster than we did."[22] The fact is, however, that few organizations have workforces that truly participate in management decisions. Given the overwhelming data that this practice produces better results, it is surprising that so few companies do it. A Christ-based leader who makes everyone a leader must take the attitude that he or she does not have all of the answers and that "ordinary" workers should not only be listened to, but given pertinent, understandable information about company policies and finances that influence their work. Some CEOs fear that adopting this philosophy will be perceived by some as giving up power. The reality, however, is that by such a practice one does not give up power, but wisely apportions it. The key, in Welch's words, is "to have the right people solving problems, no matter where they are located geographically or hierarchically."[23] As Christians, we should intuitively understand that every employee has value and a purpose. The apostle Paul says, "In humility consider others better than yourselves. Each of you should look not only to your own interests, but also to the interests of others" (Phil. 2:3-4). I remind myself of this every day by reading a note, taped permanently to my desk, that asks, "What have I learned from others today?"

The following is a real-life example of how taking the time to create a participatory workforce can have a positive impact on a company's bottom line. At an upscale steakhouse, the manager noticed that customers were sending back to the kitchen an unacceptable number of steaks that had been grilled too long. These had to be thrown out, and the chef had to start over. The manager had a couple of options. He could call the kitchen staff to his office and berate them for being careless about the distinction between "medium" and "medium well." Or he could provide them with sufficient information about why getting it right the first time is so important, and ask them to come up with a solution. He chose the latter approach. He called the staff together for a meeting and wrote at the top of a flip chart the average amount of food revenue per customer the restaurant received each evening ($20.45). He then subtracted the daily per-customer costs of overhead ($6.10), labor ($5.95), and side dishes ($1.45). This left $6.95. The average steak cost the restaurant $6.15. If all went smoothly, the restaurant would make 80¢ on a bill of $20.45 per customer. But if a steak is returned and thrown out, and another must be prepared, the restaurant stands to lose $5.35. This meant that, for the restaurant to turn a profit, it would take seven additional customers to make up for that one tossed steak. The manager reminded his staff that the restaurant has to make a profit to stay in business and to be able to give regular raises. The staff was amazed at how slim the profit margins were for the restaurant. They had been working under the assumption that the owners were easily getting rich from their venture. After the manager's presentation, a productive conversation led to many ideas as to how every member of the staff could help ensure that steaks are cooked to the customer's satisfaction. Among the solutions was a commitment on the part of the wait-staff to carefully explain the distinctions in a steak's cooking time, and an effort on the part of the kitchen staff to better gauge preparation time to match the customer's expectations for a good steak. For the first time, employees completely understood the financial ramifications of their mistakes, and felt empowered to take corrective action.

For a leader to make everyone a leader, he or she must continually strive to create "transparency" within the organizational culture. Transparency means letting go of command-and-control methods, and creating instead an atmosphere of openness and trust. It means creating a culture and opportunity for all voices within the organization to be heard. It also means sharing all relevant information with customers, employees, and shareholders, so that everyone connected with the organization is enabled to make good, informed decisions. These are all key aspects of being a servant-leader.

I work with the philosophy that there are no organizational secrets, and that everyone should have access to and understand our financial data and goals. In order to attract and retain the best and the brightest employees, it is imperative to develop a culture that allows everyone to become a leader and create value. We do this by helping our subordinates balance their professional and their personal lives; by giving them opportunities for personal and spiritual growth; by holding them accountable for their actions and decisions; and by helping them understand their purpose in life and how their role in the organization is an aspect of the fulfillment of this purpose. What we receive in return is a loyal colleague and a shared commitment to the goals and vision of the organization. This strategy will be developed further in later chapters.

Adaptive Challenges

There is no question that being a business or organization leader in today's world is an increasingly challenging task. Over the past decade, article after article has hammered at us with talk of the new economy, changes in external market forces, the risk of additional terrorist attacks, and heightened customer and employee expectations. As a result, our organizational world has been turned upside down. Companies today are learning that they must adapt to instant change, and are realizing that operating under a five-year strategic plan is about as effective as reading tea leaves. Company executives have also felt the heat when their boards of directors impatiently demand that they produce immediate results. Shareholders likewise demand constant growth and will severely punish companies for satisfying merely 95 percent of their expectations. Leadership guru Tom Peters recently wrote an article in *Fast Company* titled, "Leadership Is Confusing As Hell." In it, he puts a playful spin on the agitated state of business today and how being a leader in the next five years will bring even more surprises. He observes, "It's only going to get weirder, tougher, and more turbulent."[24]

But in these uncertain times, a Christian leader has a unique advantage. It is an undisputed fact that leaders and organizations must learn new ways of doing business and new ways to compete if they are to survive and thrive in the twenty-first century. What is required of a leader in today's business environment? The most accurate and helpful description I have found is what Ronald Heifetz labels "adaptive challenges."[25] Heifetz talks about how a leader must mobilize an organization to "adapt its behaviors in order to thrive in a new business environment." But, being adaptable, as Heifetz describes, is a daunting task for two reasons. First, it means having to change our individual style of leadership. We are no longer being called on to provide solutions, but to harness the collective intelligence of our employees at all levels and across all boundaries in order to problem-solve. Second, it means understanding that, while adapting to change is hard for an organization's leader, it is even harder on employees. Employees "often look to the senior executive to take problems off their shoulders. But those expectations have to be unlearned."[26]

A leader in an adaptive situation needs to stand above the fray and identify the challenge. She needs to manage stress and maintain focus. Finally, she needs to let the work be done by the workers who can most effectively do it, and to listen to and protect the voices of leadership that emerge from the lower branches of the hierarchy. These tasks, which are tasks of a servant leader, should come easily to Christian leaders, because the characteristics of a servant leader flow naturally from Christian beliefs.

Several years ago I was thrown into an adaptive leadership situation. I was only thirty-five years old and had not had the benefit of reading Heifetz or engaging in extensive formal management training. I was pretty much left to my own devices. Our $30 million organization was bleeding to the tune of $1 million a year, we were down to about $2 million in the bank, our credit sources were drying up, and the marketplace was rapidly deteriorating before our eyes. Managed care was making some of our programs obsolete and other programs unprofitable. We realized that in a time when the market required us to be specialized, we were, in fact, generalists. We had a top-down budget process, which resulted in our program and facility managers not owning the end product (and in some cases not even knowing what the end product was). We had an organizational culture that discouraged risk-taking and encouraged "yes men" (and women). Serious backbiting was taking place, and there was little trust among our management group.

Three years and a lot of sweat and sleepless nights later, we had developed a unified management team, a clear strategy of where we were going, an operational plan that was developed from the bottom up, a budget that almost doubled in size, and an average yearly fund-balance gain of more than $1 million. This, despite the fact that, because of our mission and purpose, two-thirds of our some thirty programs are designed to lose money. How did we do it? Heifetz would say that we had developed "the organizational and cultural capacity to meet problems successfully, according to our values and purposes."[27] And he is right. By standing back and identifying the challenges, managing stress, maintaining focus, apportioning power wisely, and listening to leadership voices from all levels of the hierarchy, we turned our organization around. We followed sound Christian leadership strategies that included incorporating the principles of servant leadership from the bottom up, creating a healthy culture that valued its employees. We created a realistic and comprehensive strategic plan that defined what we were capable of doing well; we abandoned programs in which we no longer had the expertise that today's market demanded, and emphasized quality services and products above everything else. We listened to employees' suggestions and concerns, and demanded that people be held accountable. In other words, we became leaders.

Our shared values helped us adapt to the challenges we faced. Having Christians on our leadership team did not make our decisions any easier. Losing $1 million a year feels lousy regardless of your religious beliefs. But our shared values and belief systems were instilled in our strategic plan and our organizational culture, providing us with a framework for making difficult decisions. Not everyone responded well to this new culture. Some left on their own. Others were asked to leave when it became clear that their values were not compatible with those of the organization. Those who chose to stay, however, melded into a cohesive organizational family that has eagerly welcomed like-minded leaders to join them. We received some criticism from well-meaning supporters who were of the opinion that closing programs and laying off employees was counter to the mission of a Christian organization. But in the end, we never wavered from our first responsibility, which is to add long-term value to the communities that we serve. That is both good business and good stewardship.

Leadership Is Not Confusing As Hell!

At this point, I must respectfully state that I disagree with Tom Peters—leadership does not have to be confusing, frustrating, or lonely, even in the midst of adaptive challenges. If carried out systematically and within a Christian framework, leadership can not only produce good business results, it can also be rewarding and fun. As an added bonus, it might even allow for quality time with family. Being a Christ-based leader adds value to society and makes the lives of those around us at work and at home richer and more meaningful.

Leadership, in essence, is pretty straightforward stuff. Christian leaders serve as role models, they create a vision to help people pursue goals larger than themselves, they care for people, they listen, they mentor, and they reward results. To accomplish this, we need to reclaim personal authenticity and integrity as the most powerful tools in our arsenal. In the words of U.S. House Majority Leader Tom DeLay, "It is your Christian principles and values that provide you the foundation to do well."[28] We also need to adopt a framework that is consistent with a values-based philosophy and that allows us to add long-term value to our organization. My philosophy of leadership is not confusing at all. With the golden rule at its heart, it is quite simple and has allowed me to inculcate Christian values within my organization in order to achieve our shared vision and goals.

The Final Test

There are two final questions one must ask along the road to becoming a true servant-leader: Do I know when it is time to leave my organization? Have I ensured that my organization will be better off in my absence than if I had stayed?

The first is, by far, the harder of the two questions. Determining when is the best time to leave requires discernment and honest self-examination. The decision to remain or to leave cannot be arrived at on the path of self-interest or convenience. It cannot be based on criteria driven by personal matters, such as financial security or what year one's youngest child will leave the nest. Knowing when to leave requires much prayer and honest answers to two more questions: Am I continuing to add real value to the organization? Am I still the best person for the job? If the answer to either question is no, it is a leader's responsibility to make a transition into the next chapter of his life. Only in this way can he remain authentic as an individual. Admittedly, the process one goes through to answer these questions is often gut-twisting and soul-wrenching. It requires a willingness to engage in painful self-examination and to get second opinions from friends, enemies, coaches, colleagues, and spouses. It requires putting others' interests ahead of one's own. In some situations, it may even require "predicting" the answer two or three years into the future in order to begin a proper transition process.

During the past year, as I considered the two questions, my answer to the first was "yes." I truly believed that I continue to add value to my organization. My answer to the second question, however, was leaning more toward an eventual "no." After prayer and contemplation, I arrived at the decision that, in two or three years, my organization would be better off under the leadership of another person. I began to think and plan with trusted colleagues and board members about what might be the most effective transition process. The board and I realized that our chief operating officer possessed most of the right qualities to succeed me, and, in some areas, had more talent than I ever hoped of having. In other areas, however, he still lacked crucial experience. At the same time that we were quietly gathering names of candidates outside our organization, we were also preparing this man as a potential successor. As part of his training process, we sent him to the American Management Association's Course for Presidents. Upon returning, he suggested that he begin a 360 evaluation, to which I agreed, assuring him that he need not share the results with me. Out of his sense of our mutual trust and character-based relationship, he chose to do so. As a result, we worked together to create a training program to help him improve his skills.

I am confident that by the end of our transition process, I will have left the organization in the hands of a leader who truly has the "entire package," and who, in many ways, has the potential to do a better job as CEO than I. I will have accomplished my goal of making the organization stronger in my absence than in my presence. Will it be hard to leave an organization where they will do just fine without me? Yes. Upon reflection, though, I feel this is my most important accomplishment during my tenure as CEO, because it ensures that the organization will remain strong for years to come.

The Challenge

Before sending his disciples into the mission fields, Jesus exhorted them: "I am sending you out like sheep among wolves. Therefore be as shrewd as snakes and as innocent as doves" (Matt. 10:16). This statement sums up the characteristics of a successful leader. It recognizes the value of "idealism tempered by realism, principles laced with shrewdness, integrity married to astuteness: precisely the qualities that leaders need."[29] In the following chapters, we will explore in greater detail the best practices and research of those who lead for the long term—those who follow the Golden Rule of Leadership, and who are intent on creating lasting change and value in their organizations.

To lead takes an unwavering commitment to faith and the new possibilities and promises of each new day. Over the long term, what separates a great leader from the rest of the pack is the ability continually to reinvent an organization, a career, and a life in a manner that is pleasing to God. The rewards of effective leadership can be measured tangibly in terms of organizational growth, of the quality of goods or services provided, and in the difference the organization makes in the lives of clients, customers, and employees. The intangible, but most rewarding, benefit is the quiet satisfaction that comes from making the most of one's God-given abilities and with sleeping well at night.

chapter two

create an effective organizational culture

So in everything, do to others, what you would have them do to you.
—Matthew 7:12

Organizations that do not value their employees in today's competitive environment will simply not be around for long. A leader has the responsibility to design purposefully and systematically an organizational culture in which employees are truly valued while achieving the long-term goals of the organization. Such a culture requires a framework that allows for hiring and retaining good employees, creating a vibrant and values-based organizational community, letting employees know they are part of a larger purpose, and aligning the interests of employees with those of the organization. This chapter offers strategies for creating such a culture. The key, once again, as Christians, is to following the Golden Rule of Leadership. Jesus, through his teachings, provides a strategy that will, over the long term, add lasting value to any organization.

It's Not Your Father's World
It is much harder to retain skilled people today than it was even five years ago. The reasons behind this flow from three converging

realities. First, workers have collectively, for decades, experienced organizations that neglect to follow the golden rule. Employees discovered that they were asked to commit body and soul to the company, but the company did not commit itself to them. This has resulted in workers who are less loyal to the organization, more mobile, more wary, and more demanding. Because they feel disenfranchised, workers today are letting it be known that if the company cannot promise them a job for life, they will make other demands to compensate. Second, a changing labor market has emerged in the United States. Not only is it more difficult to find and keep good employees, but the global economy has made our world smaller, and requires employees to be more skilled, possess better people skills, and perform at a higher level. As a result, it is harder to find employees that meet these increasingly demanding criteria. Third, members of generation X are filling the workforce. While they are enthusiastic about their careers, they are more restless and less likely to stay with one company for an extended number of years. These three realities have produced employees, young and old, who realize that they work for themselves, not for the company. The good news, however, is that today's workers *can* be loyal. But an organization must earn that loyalty.

Organizations have come to recognize that they must change in order to survive in today's market. When I began my professional career two decades ago as a young attorney at a Chicago law firm, the organizational culture demanded much of its employees, but seemed to care little about them. The unspoken work ethic was to conform to conservative standards, work long hours, and do whatever your managing partner said. In return, you would be fairly compensated (not, however, if you calculated your pay by the hour) and, if you were lucky, be considered for promotion to junior partner in seven years. If the promotion did not become a reality, you were asked to leave. We may think it surprising today that there was little turnover. But lawyers then had fewer expectations than they do today. They accepted this work arrangement as part of the culture at the time.

Fast-forward to the year 2000. The cream-of-the-crop, silk stocking, Wall Street legal and investment firms were being forced to transform their cultures overnight. Faced with substantial defections of their employees to the dot.com market, Wall Street firms had cultural change thrust upon them by lower-level employees seeking their fortune. Philip J. Purcell, chairman of Morgan Stanley Dean Witter, Inc., put it simply at an annual shareholders meeting: "We cannot attract the best minds with a formal dress code."[1] That same day, Salomon Smith Barney, Inc., not only gave their junior analysts more pay, but also laptop computers, gym memberships, more dinner money, and brokerage discounts.[2] If these venerable firms have made sweeping organizational changes in line with today's culture, it is a sure thing that your organization will as well. What these companies seemingly still failed to realize, however, is that over the long term, employees cannot be "bought." As will be demonstrated, employees will only be loyal and productive if they feel valued, their jobs have meaning, and they are treated under the principle of the Golden Rule of Leadership.

Today's Employees Are Paid Volunteers

Leaders today need to redefine the concept of "employee." Historically, many organizations looked upon employees as mere commodities to be used and disposed of—human resources. Employees came to work, did their jobs, got paid, and went home. And if they did not fill the bill, there were ten more lined up outside to take their place. But this is no longer the case. In today's society, employees are in the driver's seat. They have been empowered. They can make choices. They can click on to the Internet twenty-four hours a day and find out what jobs are available in any city of the country, and what those jobs are paying. In a speech to nonprofit leaders, Jeffrey Swartz, president and CEO of the Timberland Company, a for-profit company, perceptively described his employees in the following manner:

We have paid volunteers at Timberland, the same as you have docents in your museums, the same as you have volunteers who stuff envelopes, the same as you have passionate people who choose to spend their time with you. Either people choose to spend their time at Timberland, or they can go anywhere they want instantly. . . . They have the authority and they have the opportunity to make moral choices.[3]

Many leaders have not grasped fully the significance of what Swartz says: employees are, in fact, paid volunteers who have both the authority and opportunity to make moral choices. The reality is that many leaders do not make it a priority to create a meaningful and humane culture for their employees. They may strive to make a difference, implement ideas, serve clients, build a better product, get rich, or obtain power. But more than anything on a leader's plate at a given moment, creating an effective culture for employees, under the tenet of the golden rule, may be the most difficult and the most important. As leaders, we must ask ourselves: "How do I invest in my organization's culture in order to support organizational success?" The answer is surprisingly simple—the Golden Rule of Leadership. This means embracing the idea that the employment contract is a two-way street. We as leaders are right to have expectations of our employees. But those expectations must be counterbalanced by the value we place upon our employees themselves. If the scale is not even, something is wrong.

Applying the golden rule requires that we take a comprehensive inventory of employee needs. Do my employees feel they are working for a cause greater than themselves? Do they feel they are being treated fairly? Does the organization truly listen to their ideas and dreams? In what ways would the organization be of help to them should a family emergency arise? Do they have any close friends in the organization? Do they get the sense that we are investing in them for long-term, individual success? A recent study found that most companies were not successfully answering these questions. Hudson Institute and Walker Information surveyed three thousand workers. Fifty-six percent said they felt their employers failed to show any concern for them; 45 percent said they were not treated fairly; and 41 percent said they did not feel their employer trusted them. In essence, organizations were not adhering to the golden rule. Not surprisingly, only 24 percent of those surveyed indicated that they were truly loyal to their company.[4]

Other relevant research includes a study by Watson Wyatt Worldwide, a benefits consulting firm that measured company employee practices. They concluded that companies with the best employee business practices in such areas as communications, integrity, and the creation of a collegial, flexible workplace, had a 28 percent shareholder return in the first six months of 1999. Companies that fell in the middle two quartiles of these business practices showed a 12 percent return.[5]

There is no one-size-fits-all answer for fixing organizations that perform poorly in this regard. Underlying the golden rule, however, are several philosophical tenets that can drive a successful strategy. The remainder of this chapter will focus on the building blocks of an effective Christ-based organizational culture that is attentive to the needs of the organization while applying the golden rule in employee relations.

Build a Cause

It is of primary importance for an organization to create a cause that is larger than the employee. As Christians, we intuitively understand the desire to lead a life of significance. Viktor Frankl, the Austrian psychiatrist, writes: "Success, like happiness, cannot be pursued; it must ensue . . . as the unintended side effect of one's personal dedication to a cause greater than oneself."[6] Almost all of us have to work for a paycheck, and how much money we make matters. But our experience tells us that we will work harder if we believe we are working for more than just money.

The longest days I ever put in were when I worked for Governor Michael Dukakis's presidential campaign. I took a significant salary cut—to $22,000 a year—and was willing to work seven days a week, living in eight apartments across seven cities in one year, all because I believed in the individual and in our collective potential to make a difference in the world. In the same way, I am willing to work on this book at 9:00 P.M. in a hotel room with the hope that what I have to say may make a difference in someone else's life. I call this having a purpose.

Our employees also crave purpose in their professional lives, beyond merely their desire for a paycheck. Creating a purposeful culture begins by clearly defining the values and vision of an organization. The next step is to create a cause that can provide meaning to an employee's life. Employees are motivated by goals that are bigger than the company's bottom line—goals such as making the world a better place, improving the health of a community, providing great customer services, or improving the lives of their colleagues. These matter more to employees than corporate goals that are not in sync with the employee's passions. Albert Siu, former chief learning officer of AT&T, comments, "A company that doesn't act upon its espoused core set of values, and is not driven by a cause, is akin to a person without a soul and aspirations."[7]

Tom Peters describes it this way:

> If you want people to care—really to care—enlist them in a cause that they can care about: being part of the team that will go down in history for inventing the most amazing personal computer that the world has ever seen (Apple's Mac); achieving customer loyalty so intense that it becomes the stuff of legends (Nordstrom); executing a strategy with such precision that proud old competitors are publicly humbled in the market (Home Depot). People enlist on behalf of a cause. They do the impossible for a cause. For a business, however, they just work. What's your cause?[8]

Merck Pharmaceutical states its cause publicly: "We are in the business of preserving and improving human life. All of our actions must be measured by our success in achieving this goal."[9] Merck correctly understands that there is a direct connection between building a culture around successfully "preserving and improving human life" and having a positive bottom line. Leaders there know that if they are successful at achieving the former, the latter will follow suit.

The following is an example of a company that "didn't get it." Before the breakup of the Bell System in 1984, AT&T employees had a reason to come to work every day. It was their purpose to provide telephone service to the entire country—rural and urban, rich and poor—and to be the leader in providing the nation with the best communication system in the world. This is what helped them attract and keep talented people, and it is why investors invested in the company. According to David Isenberg, former AT&T strategist, none of the CEOs who came to AT&T after the breakup addressed what the company's new purpose might be. "Nobody managed the culture after there was no longer a reason to come to work," said Isenberg. As a result, talented employees left in droves, current employees have no driving purpose, customers do not understand what kind of company they are dealing with, and investors have no reason to buy AT&T stock.[10]

I once knew a CEO of a publishing company who bragged about how he was teaching his managers to be "bastards." Similarly, according to early reports, Daimler-Chrysler is another company that does not appear to understand that truly caring about its employees is the only way to ensure long-term success. Speaking at an industry conference in Strasbourg, France, Eckhardt Cordes, a top Daimler-Chrysler executive, argued that the key to boosting the company's performance in America was to implement a "traditional management approach: tough, direct, and no mercy."[11] I would not choose to work at an organization that practices this philosophy; I would not want to be its customer, nor would I invest in such a company.

Contrast these examples with Charles Schwab, a company that took another route. It focused on meeting the needs of its customers and employees, rather than maximizing short-term company profit. Schwab based its organizational culture around the mission that it was their job to provide customers with the most useful and ethical financial services in the world. David Pottruck, president and co-CEO of Schwab, tells of how founder Charles Schwab could talk for hours about the opportunity to serve others and make a difference, and never once mention profits. Pottruck lists four reasons that Schwab emphasizes in its organization's culture:

1. it grounds people in something that is unchanging
2. it builds a basis of alignment—a single direction toward which to move
3. it serves as a filter for determining who is "with us," and who is not
4. it helps export company values to customers

Schwab felt that instilling such a culture was important enough to spend $6 million on one Saturday in 1999 to gather five thousand employees in San Francisco, and link another eight thousand worldwide through video-simulcast, to hear Schwab and Pottruck discuss their corporate values and philosophy. The payoff for this impressive effort was a drop in employee attrition from 13 to 11 percent. That is a significant decrease, given that company estimates place a $15 million price tag on every percentage point caused by attrition. In effect, Schwab had invested $6 million in their employees to save $30 million.[12] This bears out the findings of Watson Wyatt Worldwide, which showed that companies with highly committed employees enjoy a much higher return to shareholders.[13]

Let me share with you another stellar example in which a company created a positive culture based on the Golden Rule of Leadership. Thrivent Financial for Lutherans is a Fortune 300 financial services company. Its clientele comprises 2.4 million

Lutheran families and individuals, with more than $57 billion in assets. Thrivent is unique in that it returns a portion of its profits back to its clients, as well as to Lutheran congregations and organizations. Thrivent's purpose as an organization is to help "Lutherans link faith, values, and finances." This is their niche in an arena that includes such competitors as Northwestern Mutual, Merrill Lynch, and Charles Schwab.

In early 2000, through a collaborative process, Thrivent (then known as Lutheran Brotherhood)[14] developed new values statements for its employees that include the following notion: "Members first, treat others with respect and dignity, keep your promises, act with integrity, and show genuine concern for others." The company posted these statements throughout home and field offices and created a section on their Intranet site for employees to give "testimonials" as to how they emulated these values. The site also gives employees opportunities to discuss how they believe a particular company policy or action contradicts the values statements. Thrivent believes that in order to make its values come alive, it has to address its mistakes publicly—with the understanding that they will correct them—while also celebrating their successes. By developing an inclusive and caring culture, Thrivent has attracted and retained gifted financial planners, some of whom have turned down six-figure signing bonuses with competitors. Employees believe in the organization's mission, morale is at an all-time high, and performance results surpassed previous records. Beth Fratzke, a Thrivent employee, pays the organization her highest compliment: "It's because of the values, that an Italian-American Presbyterian from Nebraska, with an amiable-driver personality, can actually feel at home at [Thrivent]."[15]

Give Back to the Community

Most people would agree that every organization, for-profit or nonprofit, has a moral obligation to be responsible socially and to improve the quality of the communities in which they do business. What company leaders do not often realize is that following the golden rule in terms of an organization's relationship with the community can also be good for the company's bottom line. Practicing this philosophy makes an organization stand noticeably apart from the competition, and it provides another opportunity to deepen the bond between the organization and its employees. Carried out properly, community involvement programs can have an impact on the hiring, retention, and loyalty of employees, as well as on marketing and sales results.

One company that does an effective job of incorporating its social conscience into its strategic plan is Target. The organization has a strategic goal to give back, to each community in which it operates, 5 percent of all profits, or a total of $2 million every week nationwide. The company markets this strategy effectively throughout its stores. Employees feel proud working hard for Target, knowing that bigger company profits will translate into more money for the women's shelter down the street. Customers also feel good that they are part of a greater cause in that their community benefits every time they shop at Target.

Similarly, LensCrafters, Inc., has the "Gift of Sight" program in which employees volunteer to travel throughout the United States and around the world to give free eye exams and eyeglasses to those who cannot afford them. Patagonia, Inc., a maker of outdoor wear, contributes 1 percent of its gross sales to environmental causes. In 1998, that amount surpassed $10 million. Rejuvenation Lamp & Fixture Company strives to balance the impact it has on the environment with its need to be financially viable by founding and supporting a nonprofit organization that builds "an ecologically and economically sustainable society." Other for-profit organizations, like Marriott Hotels, have found that allowing employees time off to volunteer in their local communities is good for their corporate image, as well as for employee morale. Another standout example is Avon, which has successfully coupled its volunteer program with its cause-related marketing campaign that focuses on breast-care awareness.[16]

Successful companies realize that including the entire organization in giving back to the community empowers employees by making them feel they are a part of the solution. Corporate programs aimed at helping communities ultimately have a positive influence on the bottom line by building loyalty, improving employee morale, and providing an effective way to attract and keep valued customers.

Turnover

Brad Hewitt, former CEO and president of Diversified Pharmaceutical Services, describes the "problem" of turnover when he says: "Companies don't have a shortage-of workers problem, they have a good-place-to-work problem."[17] An organization's success at employee retention has a direct impact on its ability to create value. A survey of more than 250 executives ranked customer satisfaction and employee retention as the two most important components for creating long-term value within an organization—more important even than cultivating image, revenue growth, market share, technology investment, and product development. The majority of executives surveyed also admitted that they were not doing enough in these areas.[18]

A study recently reported in *The Wall Street Journal* estimates that it costs $34,100 for an information-technology company to replace each lost programmer or systems analyst, and $10,445 for each sales clerk "lost" in specialty retail stores. The article further reported that for each lost employee at call centers and fast-food stores, the cost is $6,926 and $1,520 respectively.[19] Sibson and Company, a consulting firm studying high-turnover industries like specialty retail, call centers, high-tech and fast-food industries, found that turnover costs depressed company earnings and stock prices an average of 38 percent. These costs included money for recruiting, advertising, headhunting, and training, as well as processing out the departing employee.[20]

Companies can decrease turnover by adhering to the Golden Rule of Leadership. Take Starbucks Corporation as an example. Howard Schultz, the company's CEO and chairman, states: "It's an ironic fact that while retail and restaurant businesses live or die on customer service, their employees have among the lowest salaries and worst benefits of any industry. These people are not only the heart and soul but also the public face of the company. Every dollar earned passes through their hands." Schultz goes on to ask, "Can you afford to treat him or her as expendable?" Starbucks makes itself the retail employer of choice by providing wages that are higher than the industry average, generous benefits, health insurance for all workers, including part-time employees, and stock options. The result? Employee turnover is far below industry average—60 percent to 65 percent a year, compared to anywhere from 150 percent to 400 percent in the restaurant industry. In addition, the turnover rate among store managers is about 25 percent, half the industry average.[21] As another example, Deloitte & Touche estimates that it saved $10.6 million in 1997 by lowering its turnover rate for professional women by just 2.5 percent. The company estimated that, on average, it would cost 1.5 times the employee's annual salary to recruit and train a replacement.[22]

As Christians, we naturally desire to care for our fellow human beings, and this includes those who work for us. Taking care of our employees by following the golden rule is the right thing to do, and it makes good financial sense. As the data demonstrates, the tension between people's needs and profit obligations disappears when an organization adheres to the golden rule.

Hire Employees with Like-Minded Principles

The best employee benefit program, compensation plan, and compelling mission will not matter if you do not initially hire the "right" people. Schultz, of Starbucks, places great importance in an individual's "values" when hiring a new employee:

Whether I'm hiring a key executive, selecting an investment banker, or assessing a partner in a joint venture, I look for the same kind of qualities most look for in choosing a spouse: integrity and passion. To me, they're just as important as experience and abilities. I want to work with people who don't leave their values at home but bring them to work, people whose principles match my own. If I see a mismatch or a vacuum where values should be, I prefer to keep looking.[23]

Southwest Airlines' sophisticated hiring system helps ensure that new employees fit within its organizational culture. In 1999, Southwest interviewed 80,000 people to fill 4,200 job openings. Each candidate went through a vigorous interview process that lasted up to six weeks. Twenty percent of those hired did not make it beyond the training period. The payback, according to Libby Sartain, vice president for people for Southwest, is that the company is able to maintain a self-monitoring culture of self-motivated employees, low turnover, and high-customer satisfaction.[24] Finding the "right" employees for an organization is critical, and "right" is determined as much by shared values as it is by skills and experience.

Similarly, Ed Kruse, chairman of Blue Bell Creameries, and Merle Borchelt, former CEO of Central and Southwest Corporation, have both told me that a person's values and work ethic are the two primary factors they focus on when making hiring decisions. As Christian leaders, it is natural to lift up both our own values and those of our organizational culture during the interview process in order to uncover information about an interviewee's values. When a company adheres to the golden rule, it is committed to hiring individuals who share its values, thereby enhancing the organization's culture for the long term.

Focus on Your Key Employees

Historically, companies viewed their manufacturing process as primary, and its workers, for the most part, as interchangeable. Today, it is the reverse: For many organizations, the employee is primary and the technology is interchangeable. If a significant portion of an organization's success depends on the intellect and ability of employees, it follows that managing the company's culture is paramount. Placing particular focus on key employees is a necessary aspect of such management.

I live in Austin, Texas, home of companies like Dell, Tivoli, Vignette, and a host of other high-tech leaders that transformed our sleepy university and state government town into the Silicon Valley of the south. Many of these start-up firms have found that, while they may excel in their technology, it is the human factor that will make or break them. In a culture that relies heavily on the Internet, it is people, not technology, who provide a company's competitive advantage and leverage point.

James Copeland, Jr., CEO of Deloitte Touche Tohmatsu, says new technology allows intellectual ideas to be leveraged quickly into the marketplace, enabling a company to create value rapidly. Thus, retaining key people is vital for creating stakeholder and shareholder value. Copeland uses the term "personal value creation" in describing how to keep key employees. He further comments that, while money is important, companies must also provide employees with opportunities to enhance their intellectual capital. An organization must develop an atmosphere of mutual trust, be committed to quality, and have a nurturing environment.[25]

It is vital in today's economy to target key employees—those it would be difficult to replace—and create a separate retention plan for that group. And, while adequate compensation is important, it only gets you a ticket to the game. It is a given that your pay scale should be competitive, but other factors are also of considerable importance. Steve Ballmer, CEO of Microsoft, puts it simply: "Know your key employees and dedicate yourself to their well-being."[26] Key employees need to feel they create value and work for a cause that is larger than themselves. They must have opportunities for career development and career management. Key employees want to take pride in the organization and work with interesting people who treat them with respect, and they prefer to be supervised by a mentor, as opposed to the boss in a traditional hierarchy.

Leaders must tailor-make strategies for each key employee, based on individual needs. In my own organization, there are two key executives that report directly to me. Both of these individuals are critical to our long-term success. Without them, it is likely that our organization would miss opportunities to add millions of dollars of value. I worked with each person separately, heard what they saw as their long-term career goals (one wants to succeed me as CEO; the other set his sights on eventually becoming a leader of a different type of nonprofit organization), set up a training program to help each move toward these goals, and locked them into a four-year golden handcuff contract that promises rewards if they stay and financial penalties if they leave early. This agreement works because they had trust in me as their leader, and because it was crafted in a way that was mutually beneficial to them and to the organization. Similarly, each senior manager in our organization is asked to be fully dedicated to the well-being of his or her team. We closely track our intentional retention efforts. In 2002, our retention rate for the top sixty managers was more than 90 percent.

Good Management Is Mandatory

In a twenty-five-year period, the Gallup Organization has compiled interviews with more than a million workers. Using data from these interviews, Marcus Buckingham and Curt Coffman persuasively demonstrate that the quality of the relationship between employees and their direct supervisors is the single most important variable in creating a healthy organizational culture. In their book, *First Break All the Rules: What the World's Greatest Managers Do Differently*, they show that the quality of that relationship directly influences employee loyalty and productivity, for better or for worse. The authors say that workers seek internal and emotional satisfaction from their supervisors. They want to know clearly what is expected of them and that they are valued. They want a direct supervisor who encourages them to grow and develop. When such qualities are absent in a manager, employees begin to look elsewhere. As Buckingham and Coffman put it, "People leave managers, not companies."[27]

Does Compensation Matter?

As I have already suggested, every organization struggles with the issue of appropriate compensation. Some mistakenly believe that paying high salaries eliminates the need to focus on other aspects of creating a healthy organizational culture. Others underestimate the actual cost of not paying a fair wage. In my experience, I have found that the same principle applies across the board with nonprofit, for-profit, and church-related organizations. Many leaders in the nonprofit arena excuse their low salary scale, claiming that to raise it would result in cutting necessary programs. They convince themselves that their employees are willing to make significant financial sacrifices because they view their jobs as personal sacrifices in the cause of serving others.

I don't buy this argument. It is too often an excuse—for poor leadership, for a lack of need for a product or service, for unwillingness to make tough decisions. Further, the argument can be used to defend poor strategic planning, a deficient understanding of the cost of missed opportunities and turnover, and shortsighted thinking. Paying inadequate salaries violates the golden rule, lowers morale, prevents organizations from attracting the best and brightest people, increases turnover, and is unfair to employee families. In my experience, following the Golden Rule of Leadership requires that compensation be competitive, taking into account geographic location, type of industry, and position within the organization. It is also wrong, however, to assume that money alone will motivate and retain workers. An aggressive compensation package is only one component of a healthy organizational culture. Employees also crave recognition for a job well done, a desire to improve their skills; they want the opportunity to make their opinions heard and to do meaningful work. Money alone cannot address those needs. As a leader, it is vital to pay attention to the full constellation of employee needs.

Employees choose to stay with an organization for specific reasons. Thomas Flannery, director of the human capital service practice at Arthur Andersen, gives two primary reasons: They want to be where the action is, and they want adequate resources. Flannery adds, "People want to feel that they're working for a winning organization. They want to feel that they have the resources to do their job. When those things don't exist, companies are forced to pay more." Chris Carlton, vice president of human resources at California-based Network Appliance, Inc., notes that senior managers must address a critical issue: "How do you make sure that people are part of the community? It's the community that's going to keep them here."[28]

The Use of Stock Options

A fairly recent phenomenon in publicly traded companies is the awarding of stock options to employees. The theory behind this practice is that stock options will help attract the most talented worker, whose sense of ownership will result in greater loyalty. This, in turn, will lead to an organization made up of people who have a common goal of creating value for the shareholder. While the intentions are good and the results sometimes successful, the use of stock options to motivate employees is fraught with peril, and may even have an adverse effect on an organization's culture.

Employers who rely on stock options to improve retention and achieve long-term goals fail to grasp how and why people are motivated to do good work and to stay with a company—reasons that have been previously discussed. Heavy reliance on stock options to attract employees can create an organizational culture that is based entirely on finance. Under this system, a worker is actually motivated to leave—once the employee gets the bonus or exercises the option, the primary goal has been achieved.

Stock options also provide executives with huge temptations to boost near-term share prices regardless of long-term consequences. During the bull market of the 1990s, ethically challenged executives at companies such as Enron and World Com used a variety of improper accounting schemes to inflate artificially earnings in an effort to keep stock prices rising. Many of these executives benefited handsomely—but wrongfully. Recently indicted World Com chief financial officer Scott Sullivan sold $45.4 million in company stock after shifting $3.9 billion in expenses to make World Com look more profitable. A more forward-thinking business leader, Laura D'Andrea Tyson, dean of the London School of Business, recommends that organizations should tailor compensation programs to base executives' rewards on performance benchmarked to the overall market or industry performance as opposed to their own stock price. Tyson also suggests that companies impose longer waiting periods between the time executives can acquire stock and sell it, and that they proactively reduce the growing gap between executive and worker compensation.[29] Leaders who follow the golden rule intuitively understand that having fair and ethical compensation systems in place increases their ability to lead. The level of disparity between executives' and workers' compensation packages directly reflects the values of an organization—and its leaders.

Management guru Peter Drucker has found that while employees across a wide range of positions find the use of stock options inadequate, it is especially unfulfilling for the "knowledge worker." He talks about a multinational Fortune 500 high-tech company that was experiencing a high turnover rate among senior researchers and technical staff. Management discovered from exit interviews that employees stated a consistent reason for leaving: "Whenever I came to talk to one of you, all you talked about was the stock price." One departing employee shared this story:

> "I spent six weeks in China with our three main customers there, and when I returned and went to the head of international technical service, I sat for an hour trying to talk about the opportunities I see in China. All that interested him was that our stock went down eight points the day before."[30]

Drucker cites Microsoft as one employer whose ex-workers leave dissatisfied, even going so far as to say they "hate" the company. According to Drucker, former employees resented the fact that top management received most, if not all, recognition. They further indicated that, because the value system is exclusively financial, they were not appropriately recognized as the scientific professionals they are.[31] Those of us who have worked in the nonprofit setting instinctively know that money is not at the top of the list of reasons why people choose to work in that sector. What *is* important for them includes the following: feeling they are not being taken advantage of financially; a sense that their work is meaningful; the knowledge that they are treated equitably and humanely; and having a clear understanding of the organization's mission and goals—as well as their individual role and objectives—and the satisfaction of knowing that they are contributing to these. Recent research by Accenture and by the Conference Board confirms this. They found that while offering employees more money does not hurt retention, compensation is not the primary reason companies lose key employees, nor is it a panacea for retaining them. Rather, they state that "limited opportunities, bad relationships with managers, and uncertain work environment are the top three reasons employees leave."[32]

It is important to create a compensation program that is in harmony with long-term goals. Compensation strategies for nonprofit organizations should be based on the appropriate market pool and on performance. Many nonprofits have implemented bonus programs for key employees, effectively placing a small percentage, usually 5 to 15 percent, of total compensation at risk. These potential bonus payments, dependent on individual and/or organizational performance, are usually paid quarterly or yearly, based on clear performance objectives that add long-term value to the organization. Publicly traded for-profit organizations should seek creative and easily understood strategies that tie compensation to long-term goals. Companies that use stock options should tie them to long-term stock performance, and should structure the entire package around a broader scope that includes customer satisfaction and employee retention. For example, Cisco Systems extended its options vesting period to five years. They also make their customers the center of their organizational culture and of its compensation strategy. A percentage of every manager's compensation is tied directly to customer satisfaction results. John Chambers, Cisco CEO, describes how effective this strategy is: "Once you say it's going to be part of their compensation, people say, 'This must really be important.'"[33]

As leaders, we must ask ourselves these questions about our organizations and the people we manage: Is compensation fair? Is the compensation system easily understood? Am I creating meaningful challenges and opportunities to keep my employees? Are they being managed in a healthy manner? What is the status of our work environment? Have employees "bought into" the organization's strategic plan, designed to lead from point A to point B? And, is achieving point B something that is meaningful to them? In other words, are we following the golden rule? Our responses to these questions provide a dependable barometer that can tell us whether we are on a track that will create long-term value in the organization.

A personal perspective
on the compensation challenge

Developing a system of compensation that is consistent with a commitment to the golden rule is the management issue I wrestle with more than any other. From a Christian perspective, national church bodies periodically issue various social justice pronouncements that provide biblical support for workers' rights to living wages and just compensation. Such thinking and guidelines are healthy and useful. Experience has taught me, however, that there is no black-and-white solution to this complex and age-old challenge. Let me outline some of the difficulties my organization faces, and some of the solutions we have evolved over time, as we have taken on this important aspect of our organizational culture.

The majority of our workers are, according to societal and governmental classifications, "unskilled." They perform necessary work. They are certified nurse assistants, cooks, home-health aides, and maids. All are tremendously important, and they are often the front line of the care given to our fragile clients.

The vast majority of these important members of our team work in our nursing homes. Most of our clients in these homes are poor, and the care that we provide is funded by the state. The state determines the per diem rate they will pay us to take care of these elderly men and women, most of whom have nowhere else to turn. The state also dictates the minimum staffing patterns for each of our facilities. As a result of these two factors—mandated per diems and staffing minimums—we are limited in our efforts to increase the revenue base for each facility, and we have limited say in controlling our labor costs, which is by far our largest expense.

When we do the math, we find that despite our best intentions, we often are unable to pay these workers what most of us would consider a living wage. We face a catch-22 situation. We can choose to pay our lower level staff members less than ideal wages, or we can choose to hurt our clients by closing the facility. We are also acutely aware that the latter choice would cause even more pain to our current staff and that any subsequent job that they might find would probably pay the same or less and would most likely (in our opinion) be with an organization that does not have as high standards as ours.

Given these real limitations, what can an organization like ours do? First, we work hard to educate the state legislature that, in a humane society, the elderly poor simply must be a budgetary priority. We have had some success in this, and increased funding goes directly to the paychecks of the direct care workers. This will, over time, improve morale and attract higher quality employees, which will translate into better care. Over the past five years the average starting salary of this level of worker in our organization has increased at a rate faster than inflation. While it is still too low, the good news is that politically and organizationally we are heading in the right direction.

In addition, unlike most of our for-profit competitors in the nursing home industry, we insist on providing health insurance to all of our employees. Access to health insurance is critical for all of us and should not be denied based on skill level. (Many, if not most, for-profit healthcare organizations circumvent laws regarding health insurance provision in a number of ways. We refuse, on principle, to follow suit). Yes, this decision has an impact on our bottom line, but it is the right thing to do even if it leaves us less profitable than some of our counterparts.

We have also made a conscious decision that, in our annual budget process, staff at the lower levels will on average receive a higher percentage raise than those at the higher levels. This is our small way of ensuring that this category of workers receives priority and that the gap between the top and the bottom does not become too great. Finally, we are constantly looking for new revenue sources that would help us to continue accomplishing our mission and increase the wages of our lower level employees.

Taking care of our employees in other ways is also a priority. Coworkers at all levels have personal and family issues that must be dealt with from time to time. At the administrative offices we regularly receive requests by administrators of specific facilities for approval of actions or expenditures that allow them to creatively address the circumstances of one or more colleagues. For example, at Christmastime, an administrator and I have worked with local Christian congregations to make sure that our clients had a Christmas complete with adequate food and gifts. But this past year, we expanded the program to include specific lower-level employees as well. We have also instituted a free tuition program that allows our more motivated lower level employees to get the training they need to advance to the next skill and pay level. We have chaplains on staff with whom employees can meet, in confidence, to seek help with personal or family issues. Facility staff members may also choose to eat, at no cost, the meals prepared in the facility's kitchen. These are just a few of the many ways our senior managers have tried to follow the golden rule while remaining within very real budgetary constraints.

Does this satisfy my qualms that our compensation strategy is fair to all of our employees? Is it biblically just that a senior manager may make up to ten times the hourly amount of an employee she supervises? The honest answer is no. What does allow me to sleep at night is the knowledge that our senior managers and I wrestle with this question daily in our ongoing efforts to come up with creative Christ-based solutions to treat all of our staff via the golden rule.

Foster Social Bonds

Another aspect of the golden rule that contributes to a successful workplace is the desire to care for one's neighbor—in this case, coworkers. Earl Maxwell, senior partner of the Austin-based accounting and financial services firm, Maxwell, Locke & Ritter, comments, "So many of our traditional communities have disappeared—neighborhoods, family structure, and churches. One way in which work can have a significant impact on peoples' lives is by building a real community within the organization, which will, in turn, also benefit the organization."[34] Surprisingly, some companies still actively discourage friendships among coworkers under the misguided belief that it will lead to too much time "goofing off," and not enough work. As mentioned earlier, one of the twelve indicators the Gallup survey listed as comprising a highly productive workplace is allowing and encouraging workers to form "best friendships." Many mergers, acquisitions, and reorganizations fail to live up to their potential for that very reason— friendship among workers is inadvertently destroyed, and this damages productivity and loyalty in the workplace. Chris Essex, a Rockville, Maryland, consultant on work-life issues, notes, "The workplace has become the social support network we used to have in our backyards over the clothesline."[35]

Southwest Airlines, known for having one of the highest-quality organizational cultures, brags about the fact that more than a thousand of its employees are now married to each other after first meeting at work. Similarly, Peter Cappelli, a professor at the University of Pennsylvania Wharton School of Business, has done research supporting the notion that building more elaborate social communities within an organization will improve employee retention. "Loyalty to companies may be disappearing, but loyalty to colleagues is not." He cites Ingage Solutions as an example of reducing turnover among mobile and marketable software engineers by creating golf leagues, investment clubs, and softball teams. Now, if employees leave, they are also leaving their primary social network. [36] As Christians, we have a unique opportunity to develop organizational communities that allow us to witness by example. It is an opportunity to put our faith into action in a manner that also furthers the mission of the organization.

Make It Fun

There is absolutely no reason that people should not have fun at work. Happy, motivated employees produce outstanding results. Management guru Oren Harari notes the connection "between smiles and discipline, laughs and focus, giggles and results, hee-haw and high performance. They are the same road."[37] A leader's attitude sets the tone for the entire organization and plays an important role in determining whether employees enjoy their jobs and are productive at work.

When I took over as CEO of a large social-service organization, morale was low. Funding cutbacks, program closures, staff layoffs, and a lack of a vision had all taken their toll. A by-product of this organizational malaise was that no one, including myself, was having much fun. Among our first priorities was to adopt an "unofficial" mission statement—*Work hard, have fun, get results*. We then communicated the message: Yes, we are going to have to work long hours in order to turn our organization around; yes, if things do not change we are going to go bankrupt; yes, results and accountability matter; and, yes, you are expected to accomplish your stated objectives or you will be asked to leave (and a few were asked). The message was blunt, but underlying it was the general understanding that life is too short not to have fun. We came to understand that working together to create a renewed organization that has a clear purpose and that makes a difference in peoples' lives is exciting and fun. Only one of our ten senior managers had trouble with the notion that you could have fun with those that reported to you, and still be an effective manager. This person left after a year, which proved best for all involved.

Examples of What Works

An attractive benefits package and employee-participation programs will not be successful if they are implemented as part of a convoluted plan to squeeze a little more work out of employees. These types of programs will only work if they are offered because it is the right thing to do. The following potpourri offers snapshots of what some companies are doing to help provide a healthy balance in employees' lives.

An outside observer might conclude that if any organization should have a turnover problem, it would be Dallas-based 7-Eleven Corporation. The company has to staff convenience stores around-the-clock throughout the nation. As part of an overall plan to help retain employees, 7-Eleven decided to provide all employees—including those we see behind the cash register—cafeteria-style medical insurance for themselves and their pets, retention bonuses based on months of work (not years), special rates on car insurance, and home security systems. Similarly, Blockbuster, Inc., is successful at keeping its college-age employees by offering tuition reimbursement and health insurance. Fidelity Investments occasionally rents space at Six Flags to entertain its employees and their families, and offers a popular concierge service that will, for example, help employees buy that last-minute gift or find those elusive Broadway show tickets.[38] Santa Clara-based Intel recently opened satellite offices in San Francisco and San Ramon to help ease the long commutes of its employees. 3Com provides valets who pick up dry-cleaning from employees' desks, and takes care of driver-license renewal. Hewlett-Packard has created virtual offices designed to encourage part-time jobs and advertise its job-sharing program.[39]

Far-sighted companies are also paying attention to workers' spiritual needs. Whitmore Manufacturing Company, based in Rockwell, Texas, has part-time chaplains on staff who hold Bible study sessions, make weekly office visits to workers, and are on call twenty-four hours a day for personal crisis situations. Whitmore contracts chaplains from Marketplace Ministries, Inc., a Dallas-based organization that, in 2000, provided contract chaplains to 236 companies in thirty-two states.[40]

Companies are also recognizing the importance of workers' physical health. Forty-one percent of companies who have more than 750 employees now have dedicated space for fitness facilities. These companies are discovering that better employee health lowers the cost of health insurance and improves job performance.[41]

While every organization's particular challenges, and every solution, are unique, what is common to every organization is the need to instill the golden rule as a core belief, as an integral part of an organization's stated values. This is the path by which to develop a work community that is properly cared for and motivated to add long-term value.

What Happens When Theory Collides with Reality?

Creating a productive organizational culture is one thing. Making difficult Christ-based day-to-day decisions that serve both your customers and your employees is where the rubber meets the road. Let me give you an example. Thrivent Financial recently implemented several family friendly policies, including a commitment that no travel on Sundays would be required. However, there are situations when client needs take precedence over employee needs. Because of the nature of its business as, among other things, money managers for 2.4 million clients, employees needed to be available when the stock market was open. That includes Christmas Eve until 2:00 P.M., as well as the Friday after Thanksgiving. Some employees felt that if the company truly claimed to be family friendly, it should also be policy to declare these days as holidays, and not require employees to work on those days.

Thrivent operates in the same environment as restaurants, hospitals, and department stores. In order to provide the best service to its customers, Thrivent needs to remain open for business on these holidays. Placing the interests of the organization first was, in the eyes of the management, vital to the creation of long-term value. The primary goal for a leader is to find solutions that simultaneously value employees *and* give customers the top priority they deserve. For example, in the case of working holidays, a skeleton staff might suffice. Or those who work might be paid time-and-a-half. Perhaps those who work a particular holiday are allowed to take off the following workday. Solutions are always specific to the situation. If properly explained and objectively implemented, the employee will respect and understand these decisions.

The same principle applies in the case if an emergency occurs at work while an employee who is needed to effect a solution is on vacation. The Golden Rule of Leadership requires the value of the vacation to be weighed against the emergency need, and an appropriate response be made—whether by telephone, E-mail, or an early return to the office. In a healthy organizational culture, responsibility is a two-way street. When the organization is in need, even the best-laid vacation plans may have to be put on hold. When the crisis is over, however, the organization has a duty to make it up to the employee who made the sacrifice. This might be by some special recognition, an eventual promotion, extra time off, or extra compensation for the missed vacation.

Following the Golden Rule in Times of Trouble

Taking care of employees who are seriously ill or who have been injured is not only the Christian thing to do, it is, in the long run, good for business. Most of us know workers or their family members who, while in their prime, were injured or diagnosed with a life-threatening disease. Crises like these make employees think about their own mortality, and the pain such an occurrence would cause their families. A good organizational culture will embrace that individual and his family and take care of them to the end, even if that employee is no longer able to be productive. This is the one and only exception to the rule that you should let a nonproductive employee go. Embracing this person and his family can be in the form of disability pay, a reduction of responsibilities without a decrease in pay, setting up a scholarship fund for the children, a liberal interpretation of the sick-day policy, even taking turns delivering meals. The goal is to care for the individual and, in so doing, demonstrate to other employees that the organization is genuinely dedicated to looking after each other in good times and bad. The short-term "cost" that your organization may incur by doing the "right thing" will be overshadowed by the long-term value you add by adhering to the golden rule.

A caring organizational culture will also provide for employees who are forced to deal with family members who are in crisis—the dying mother, the teenage son struggling with drug addiction. A healthy organization will allow extra time off for the worker to provide the help their family member needs, and other employees will pick up the missed workload. The employee will know he is being given permission—even encouraged—to take time off, trusting that leadership will not hold it against him and, even more, cares about his well-being. This again is the Christian thing to do, making it a win-win for everybody. What the organization eventually gains by practicing a philosophy of care is an employee who not only gives 100 percent, but who is deeply loyal and committed to helping the organization meet its goals.

Wall Street Takes Notice

One of the clearest indications that following the Golden Rule of Leadership translates into organizational success is the fact that Wall Street is beginning to take notice. It is well known that numerous mutual fund companies have historically frowned on investments in companies involved in the sale of tobacco products, gambling, and guns. Recently, however, managers of socially responsible investment funds have become more sophisticated in their investment scope, and have grown dramatically. It is estimated that $2.1 trillion is currently invested in funds that promote certain types of business activities. Some, like Boston-based Domini Social Investments, and Citizen's Funds, out of New Hampshire, favor companies that excel in the treatment of its workers as an investment criteria. Joe Keefe, executive vice president of Citizen's, notes: "We believe it makes good investment sense to avoid companies with sweatshop conditions and environmental problems." Robert Brady, managing director of a socially responsible investment fund for Salomon Smith Barney, comments that, "This has become a lot more mainstream than a lot of people think. . . . The market has always paid for good strategic management, and a lot of these issues are indicative of good strategic management."[42]

Next Steps

An organization is probably not creating long-term value if it has a high turnover rate and employees who feel undervalued, uncertain about expectations, and who demonstrate low energy, a "cover-your-butt" attitude, dull thinking, aversion to risk, and a need to do everything by the book. The solution in such circumstances begins by following the golden rule and establishing an organization-wide process to create a values-based culture that is aligned with a long-term strategy. Research links a golden-rule strategy and good human-capital practices with improved shareholder returns and value creation. From this, it is clear that treating employees with respect, developing their talents, and truly caring about them as fellow human beings, are critical issues in the success of your organization.

Remember how bad service on Continental Airlines used to be? Not any more. How did they do it? They recently ran ads in major newspapers throughout the country with the tag line:

Best Place to Work
Best Airline to Fly
What a Coincidence

Underneath, the ad recounts how, in 2001, Continental was named one of Fortune 100's best places to work, and was deemed "Airline of the Year" by Air Transport World. The ad goes on to state: "There's no coincidence, it's a simple formula for success, but one that makes all the difference when it comes to serving you better." It is yet one more example of how following the golden rule can add true long-term value to an organization.

chapter three

do the right thing

You can build a throne with bayonets, but you can't sit on it for long.
—Boris Yeltsin

Following the Golden Rule of
Leadership means simply to put into practice the axiom that
became the title and theme of a Spike Lee movie, *Do the Right
Thing.* This is not only biblically mandated, it is also in the best
interest of an organization. This mandate, however, runs counter
to the ever-growing economic pressure to emphasize short-term
success at the expense of ethical behavior and long-term value.
Organizations and their leaders often feel they have no choice but
to cut corners, sell a product to someone who does not really need
it, use cheaper materials, get by with an insufficient number of
employees, or use various accounting tricks as part of a convoluted smoke-and-mirrors strategy.

Still, history has shown that doing the right thing is the only
strategy that will create true long-term value. Doing the right
thing requires, simply, acting with integrity. To act with integrity,
says Stephen Carter, we must first discern what is right and what
is wrong in a given situation. Next, we must act on what we have
discerned, even if there is a personal cost involved. Finally, we
must acknowledge openly that we are acting on the basis of our
understanding of what is right and what is wrong.[1]

As leaders, we interact daily with two types of people in the professional world—those who deal with us fairly because it is the right thing to do, and those who believe that any action is acceptable as long as it is not illegal or they do not get caught. In its 2000 Organizational Survey across industries, consulting firm KPMG reported that American workers are witnessing firsthand illegal and unethical conduct at their jobs. Forty-nine percent of workers said that if these violations were made public, "significant public trust would be lost" by their company.[2] This chapter demonstrates that compromising Christian values for short-term success always costs the organization in the long term. The organization that truly cares about those it serves, that lives up to its stated values in its day-to-day actions, and that gives to employees the sense that it has its ethical priorities straight, is the organization that will be in the best position for success.

James Collins and Jerry Poras, in their seminal book *Built to Last: Successful Habits of Visionary Companies*,[3] surveyed hundreds of CEOs and asked them to identify the leading companies in their respective industries. They found that every one of the eighteen best performers considered the pursuit of high ideals to be as important as achieving a profit, and only seven of the eighteen listed maximizing shareholder returns as one of their organization's objectives. SCA Consulting, a Los Angeles-based firm, examined sixty Fortune 500 firms to see if there was a correlation between four key stakeholder indicators (corporate reputation, employee population growth, charitable giving, and inclusion) and shareholder return. They concluded that a positive correlation did exist. Michael Halloran, senior vice president of SCA, notes:

> While critics might cite companies that enjoy short-term success as a result of reducing costs at the expense of quality, eliminating employee benefits, reducing employment or curtailing their involvement in the community, there is a greater chance for producing long-term shareholder value when customers, employees, and the community are pleased with and supportive of the company.[4]

The Truth Always Comes Out

I challenge you to name one example in which unethical, illegal, and un-Christian behavior proved to be a successful long-range organizational strategy. The quote by Boris Yeltsin at the beginning of this chapter speaks volumes, whether applied to leading a nation or a business: "You can build a throne with bayonets, but you can't sit on it for long." We could fill an entire book with examples of organizations that try to "build with bayonets." But it requires only a handful of examples to demonstrate the consequences of doing so.

Anyone who has worked in a publicly held company is familiar with the pressure to meet the expectations of its analysts, along with the temptation to manipulate data to keep the stock price soaring and the value of stock options increasing. California Micro Devices, a manufacturer of semiconductor components, was not exempt from such pressure and temptation. Back in 1994, top company executives cheated customers and padded their books in a variety of ways. They recognized revenue early and shipped products to customers before they were ordered; they sent unwanted products to customers; they shipped products to freight-forwarders and counted it as sales. They faked invoices, faked customers, permitted unconditional rights of return, and created bogus title transfers. All the while they hoped that people outside the company would not notice and that no one inside would care. They were wrong.

An investigation by the Securities and Exchange Commission resulted in indictments on criminal charges against CEO Chan Desaigoudar and CFO Steven Henke. What emerged at the trial was a picture of corruption at the top, of leaders who created an organizational culture that forced people to do things they knew were wrong, but were powerless to stop due to the pressure to increase revenue. This corrupt company overstated nearly half of its recorded $38 million in revenue during fiscal year 1994. The jury foreman later commented that he was surprised at the number of people involved in the fraud. "We agreed that the fraud didn't take root at a predetermined meeting, but started from the pressures to pump up the revenue." Desaigoudar and Henke were found guilty, sentenced to thirty-six months and thirty-two months in prison, respectively, and fined a considerable amount of money. The company's stock, which had been trading at $21.25 on March 16, 1994, plummeted to $5.88 just five months later upon disclosure of the SEC investigation. When the two men were sentenced in 1998, the stock was trading at approximately $1.50.[5]

Another example is the General Motors Malibu fiasco. The company knew that the vehicle's fuel tank design was defective. Company executives decided it would be cheaper to settle any lawsuits out of court rather than spend the additional $2.40 per vehicle it would have taken to fix the problem. This was hardly a long-term, cost-effective decision. A California jury ordered the company to pay $4.9 billion (later reduced to $1.2 billion) to six people who were severely burned as a result of the defective design.[6] Then there is the case of Jacques Nasser, former CEO of Ford Motor Company, who acknowledged that quality control problems with Ford's new and redesigned vehicles cost the company more than $1 billion in lost profits in 2000, and severely hampered their growth plans.[7] Then there were the three high-level executives of Archer Daniels Midland Company who were sentenced to prison terms for their involvement in a worldwide conspiracy to fix prices of ADM products. And, of course, in the infamous Enron meltdown, stock prices collapsed from ninety dollars in August 2000 to fifty-eight cents in January 2002. The cause? Executive arrogance, less-than-forthcoming accounting practices (to put it politely), and possible criminal activity.

Marianne Jennings, professor of legal and ethical studies at Arizona State University, states plainly a fact these and other companies apparently overlooked: "The truth always gets out." Jennings uses the phrase "moment of truth" to describe the point at which a company discovers that its increased earnings are the result of faulty products or dishonest employment practices. The path an organization takes at these moments determines the true nature of its leaders. Johns Manville had its moment of truth upon learning that asbestos was causing illness among workers in the 1930s. Company executives responded by creating a strategy to prevent the scientific community from disclosing its findings about the correlation. Not an example to be emulated. Similarly, Beech-Nut was forced into such a moment when it learned—from one of its own chemists—that the company's baby products did not contain apple juice, as advertised, but rather an unadulterated chemical concoction. The moment of truth came for Kidder-Peabody when it chose to ignore warnings from employees that a glitch in the firm's accounting system resulted in bond-swaps being reported as sales and income.[8] More recently, Firestone and Ford continue to face countless lawsuits and damaging publicity by not informing the U.S. Department of Transportation that certain tires were being recalled in overseas markets due to an excessive number of rollover accidents. Both companies failed to be forthright, and the resulting damage is long term. As automotive expert Brock Yates wrote, "What we do know is that years may pass before either Ford or Firestone regains the full and complete confidence of the American public."[9]

The common denominator in all of these situations is that the companies knew they had a problem but failed to take immediate corrective action. Some hoped the problem would never be discovered. Others fired the employees who raised the issue. Each lacked the type of leader needed at a moment of truth: one who acts ethically and decisively, who goes beyond what is legally mandated, and takes whatever steps are needed to address the issue in an ethical manner. Each lacked, in other words, a leader who would choose to act with integrity and do the right thing.

As Christians, we should find it natural to be open and honest and to act with integrity. The following examples demonstrate that following the golden rule, doing the right thing, is good for business.

In the 1980s, the electric utility sector was dealing with its own potential asbestos-like issue with the public scare over the potential ill effects of electromagnetic fields on the health of people living near such facilities. The industry's response was immediate and multifaceted. Companies began including pertinent information about the issue in customer billing statements, funded outside studies and disclosed the results to customers, and encouraged every consumer and expert to study the issue. As a result, the scare has all but disappeared.

In another case, James Burke, CEO of Johnson & Johnson, ordered the immediate recall and destruction of 31 million bottles of Tylenol capsules upon learning of possible product-tampering. While the company suffered public mistrust in the short term, Johnson & Johnson eventually won back virtually all of its customers.[10]

One of the reasons Johnson & Johnson got it right was that it has a deeply ingrained organizational culture—one that has been instilled in employees since the company was founded in 1886. The company publicly states its purpose: to alleviate pain and disease. In 1935, Robert Wood Johnson reaffirmed the founding values by publicly describing his management philosophy as "enlightened self-interest," which he describes like this: "Service to customers comes first . . . service to employees and management second, and . . . service to stockholders last."[11] In 1945, Johnson & Johnson codified this philosophy in a document called "Our Credo," which is still used today. It reads, in part:
- We believe that our first responsibility is to the doctors, nurses, hospitals, mothers, and all others who use our product.
- Our second responsibility is to those who work with us.
- Our third responsibility is to the communities in which we live. We must be a good citizen—support good works and charity.
- Our fourth and last responsibility is to our stockholders. Business must make a sound profit.[12]

In the wake of the Tylenol scare, Collins and Porras aptly noted that "J & J had a codified ideology in place that guided its response to the crisis."[13] As Christian leaders, we similarly must never lose sight of the greatest possession we bring to our work: a core set of Gospel beliefs and principles that will guide us in every difficult situation we face.

Do the Right Thing When It Comes to Making the Tough Decisions

As we have already seen, doing the right thing means acting ethically, with integrity, and with regard for the long-term interests of the organization. Many well-meaning Christian leaders believe that it violates Christian principles to make decisions that will cause emotional and financial pain to employees. I do not believe the dynamic is that simple. In my view, the number-one rule of decision making is that the organization always comes first. It is only by remembering this that leaders can genuinely meet the needs of customers, employees, communities, and shareholders.

In reality, every decision that is or is not made has both positive and negative consequences. The decision maker must always balance the short-term impact of any decision on employees, customers, and the community against the potential long-term impact to the company as the result of continued financial deterioration and missed opportunities. A Christian leader has a duty to make such decisions based on Christian principles *and* the best interests of the organization. Once a decision is made, it is the responsibility of the Christian leader to use the most compassionate means to treat those affected and to support them as they rebuild their lives.

In this way, we live out the lesson learned from Jesus' parable of the talents (Matt. 25:14-30). God's servants are exhorted, in the parable, to be good stewards by multiplying the "talents" God gives us. As Christian leaders, we have been gifted with two primary abilities: to "grow" our organizations and to deal fairly and compassionately with our colleagues whose lives we influence and who share in the mission of the organization. Putting the organization first is the most effective way to "multiply talents" and keep the organization and all who are involved with it in the best possible condition.

For example, changes in the external environment may require an organization to consider moving jobs overseas, getting out of an existing line of business, closing an academic department, or shutting down an inefficient factory. Perhaps the toughest of the tough decisions is the one to let employees go, even if they are doing a great job. This has, unfortunately, become an all-too-common dilemma for leaders. In some situations, however, and carried out in the right way, downsizing can be more than just a necessary response to an organization's challenges; it can also be a Christian response.

Lawrence A. Bossidy, former CEO and chairman of AlliedSignal, Inc., once told the Economic Club of Washington, "It's not management who decides how many people are on the payroll. It's customers. . . . Without a growing roster of satisfied customers, we can all turn out the lights and go home."[14] Nasser, of Ford, states: "Given the choice, I will always reduce two jobs to save four. We don't make profits by shutting down plants."[15] Sometimes, moving some jobs overseas can actually save domestic jobs. Companies like Fruit of the Loom and Levi Strauss learned that truth too late. Analysts believe that if they had moved their factories to Mexico and Asia in the 1990s, they may have competed more effectively with companies that had already done so. Their initial intention, to save American jobs, was admirable, but the question remains whether the decision to retain domestic production actually caused employees more pain in the long run.

While there is truth in Lawrence Bossidy's comment above, layoffs can also be the unfortunate consequence of ineffective leadership. Rank and file employees have too often lost their jobs owing to poor executive decisions. There are times, however, when changes in consumer preferences or unexpected economic downturns (such as the one that followed the September 11 tragedy), make targeted layoffs necessary and vital to the long-term success of an organization. For example, changes in customer preferences caused my organization to sell several older nursing homes. Based on research, we projected that consumers would increasingly choose newer facilities, assisted living, and home-health options over the traditional nursing home model. As part of our strategic planning process, we intentionally transitioned our nursing homes and their employees to other like-minded organizations that we believed had the capacity to continue to provide this traditional type of care for the next ten years. We simultaneously added employees with different skill-sets and qualifications in order to expand our services to the elderly and meet current consumer preferences.

Simultaneously hiring and firing employees in this way can be termed a "churning" process. *The Wall Street Journal* gave this recent example: Elcotel, Inc., is a manufacturer of pay phones; their product is being made obsolete by the increasing popularity of cell phones. As a result, it had to close one of its factories, laying off seventy workers. At the same time, the company was hiring engineers and software developers to help design software to upgrade its pay phones to make them more appealing and competitive in the marketplace. Because the needed skill-sets were so different, the company felt it would be impossible to retrain employees who had worked on the now-obsolete style of phone. "You're talking about the difference between an $8-an-hour assembler and a $100,000-a-year software engineer," said CEO Michael Boyle. "The skills were not compatible."[16] Was Elcotel's decision an ethical response to the economic challenge it faced? Yes, as long as those laid off were treated fairly and compassionately—that is, in light of the golden rule. Not only did Elcotel plan strategically to meet the needs of its customers for decades to come, it also strengthened the organization for the long term by proactively making tough decisions that will benefit current and future employees.

As we consider such decisions in our own backyard, we need to be guided by our nonnegotiable Christian values. During these times I follow the words God spoke to the prophet Zechariah: "Administer true justice; show mercy and compassion to one another" (Zech. 7:9). To act in this manner, we must honestly assess our situation and learn from our past successes and failures for the sake of the future. We need to consider prayerfully all other options available—including salary reductions taken by top management—before applying any decision that involves the loss of jobs. And we need to ensure that those who are most directly effected by the decision are cared for in light of the golden rule—as we would have done unto ourselves, with mercy and compassion.

Knee-jerk responses to lay off employees during economic downturns often hurt organizations more than they help. Alan Blinder, former vice chair of the Federal Reserve Board, cites several studies to support this conclusion. He found that companies that announced large layoffs underperformed during the subsequent three-year period. A Watson Wyatt Worldwide study also found that fewer than half of the companies that downsized during the 1990 recession went on to meet their profit goals. The study also revealed that only 32 percent increased their competitive advantage, and just 21 percent reduced their inefficiency. When organizations lay off employees, leaders often fail to take into account the needs of those who remain. This oversight perhaps comes from the mistaken assumption that employees will remain loyal because they feel they are the "lucky ones" who got to keep their jobs. What often happens in these circumstances is that morale plummets, good people leave, and fewer people are left doing more work. Productivity decreases as demoralized, overburdened employees fail to work to their optimum capacity.[17] The decision to lay off employees must take into account not only the turmoil it causes in the lives of those laid off, but also the needs of those who remain at work. The goal is to retain their loyalty and improve the condition of the organization.

A growing body of anecdotal evidence shows that successful organizations are learning from mistakes made in the 1990s. Some used the 2001–2002 economic slowdown quietly to weed out underperforming employees and failing units. Others are making sure to communicate better with workers so that everyone knows how decisions are being made and when cuts will occur. One stellar example is Charles Schwab & Co., which tried to avoid layoffs by cutting the pay of its top officers and by asking 30 to 50 percent of its employees to take some Fridays off. Schwab spokesman Glen Mathison said, "You don't engender loyalty and a sense of shared mission by resorting to layoffs first."[18] A couple of months later, however, customer demand had declined so dramatically that Schwab was forced to take the next step and let some employees go. Leadership felt this was necessary to ensure the company would be financially strong in the long term. What was truly impressive about this move was the personal investment made by Charles Schwab and his wife. The couple established a $10 million fund to provide an annual tuition reimbursement of up to $10,000 for two years to any laid-off employee who returned to school.[19] Not only did the Schwabs "do the right thing," they sent a clear message that the organization truly cares about its former and current workers.

The Wall Street Journal recently chronicled the story of a company that made the effort to implement the golden rule during a difficult time. Getronics Government Solutions had to eliminate seventy of its twenty-five hundred positions, and wanted to do it as humanely as possible. Top management spent fifty days being trained in the art of breaking the news gently and dealing with workers' emotional reactions. They provided outplacement counseling, offered severance pay substantially greater than the industry norm, and made sure that the cuts did not have a disproportionate impact on women and minorities. The extra steps Getronics took cost an additional $150,000.[20] What did they get for this expenditure? The knowledge that they had treated those being laid off like they themselves would want to be treated in the same situation. The move also made a forceful and long-lasting statement to the remaining 2,430 employees: This is an organization that really cares about its employees as human beings. Only time will tell how Getronics' decision pays off. I believe that their $150,000 investment will be returned tenfold in the form of higher morale, increased productivity, stronger loyalty, and higher retention rates. The company correctly viewed the $150,000 it took to prepare its leaders for the layoff not as a short-term cost, but a long-term investment. Not only was it the right thing to do, it also made good organizational sense.

Another positive example comes from Merck, the pharmaceutical company, which made an intentional strategic move to continue to develop and distribute Mectizon at no cost to customers. This drug is effective in treating "river blindness," a disease affecting millions of people in developing countries. Even though Merck realized it stood to lose a significant amount of money by continuing to make the drug available, it remained committed to that plan because it was the "right thing to do," and because the company could afford to do it. In their analysis of this story, Collins and Porras noted that Merck also considered the demoralizing effect a decision to discontinue Mectizon would have had on its top scientists, as well as the impact of the public outcry such a decision would almost certainly inspire. In the end, Merck made its decision, trusting that such acts of goodwill "somehow . . . always pay off."[21] In the language we have been using, Merck made its decision because doing the right thing not only helped vast numbers of people, but added long-term value to the organization.

Of course, not every company has the luxury of absorbing the costs such as those taken on by Getronics and Merck. Any number of factors may preclude similar actions in a given situation. But Christian leaders participate and make decisions within a marketplace economy that creates winners and losers every day, and so have a responsibility to act with integrity and follow the golden rule in all actions. A leader must never forget that every decision has an impact on real people, and must also learn how to gauge the relationship between immediate pain and the long-term health of an organization and all its members.

Organizations that have a clear understanding of their values and purpose are better able to withstand the pressure to make short-sighted decisions, and instead, concentrate on that which truly adds value over the long term. Jim Burke, former CEO of Johnson & Johnson, describes it this way:

> All of our management is geared to profit on a day-to-day basis. That's part of the business of being in business. But too often, in this and other businesses, people are inclined to think, "We'd better do this because if we don't, it's going to show up on the figures over the short term." This document (the Credo) allows them to say, "Wait a minute. I don't have to do that." The management has told me that they're . . . interested in me operating under this set of principles, so I won't."[22]

An organization that acts with integrity also enjoys a clear competitive advantage. Don Bokenkamp, founder and CEO of Bokenkamp Drilling Company, an offshore oil-drilling company, once received a frantic phone call from the president of Chevron. He told Bokenkamp that he had an offshore oil field that needed drilling immediately, and asked him to "begin drilling tomorrow," promising that Chevron would pay "whatever Bokenkamp decided was fair after the job was completed."[23] This phone call would never have taken place if the Bokenkamp Drilling Company was not known for its quality work and its integrity as an organization.

Values at Home Also Apply Abroad
The reality of economic globalization adds to the ethical challenges that face leaders. In this world of global manufacturing, is it necessary and ethically appropriate for an organization to

move a manufacturing plant outside the country in order to pay lower, region-specific wages? I believe that in some cases it is. Such decisions have been opposed by a host of groups and individuals, including unions, political party leaders, and religious and other special interest groups. My opinion is that such moves are often inevitable in the context of our global economy and imperfect world. If carried out properly, however, the decision to move a plant outside the United States can have both domestic and international benefits. A properly executed move ultimately bears positively on the American as well as the world economy. By choosing not to move, a company may forego the opportunity to remain in step with industry costs, may lose market share, and might go out of business. Such a result indicates poor stewardship of personnel and resources.

It is just as unacceptable, however, to turn a blind eye to what takes place in overseas manufacturing plants. I, for one, did not think Nike lived up to its ethical duty to ensure that its overseas employees were treated humanely. At one point, an impressive 450,000 Asian workers produced Nike shoes. But working conditions in the Asian plants were deplorable. There were widespread reports of physical and sexual abuse of workers, inhumane working conditions, poverty-level wages (as measured in that specific region), and girls as young as thirteen working more than sixty hours a week.[24] This is unconscionable for a company that sold more than $4 billion worth of shoes in one year. Nike chose to do the wrong thing, resulting in negative press, public condemnation, diminished employee morale, lawsuits, and boycotts. Contrast Nike's actions with those of Mattel, the toy manufacturer. Mattel recently created global manufacturing principles that specifically outline requirements and prohibitions in its foreign factories. These principles address such issues as child labor, the forty-hour workweek, and the right to form unions.[25] Mattel clearly understands that doing the right thing is good for the long-term success of the organization.

Be Good Stewards of the Earth

Christian belief in the sanctity of God's creation offers another area in which leaders can set an example. Implementing the Golden Rule of Leadership with respect to environmental issues is yet another way Christian leaders can do the right thing *and* improve business.

Interface, for example, is a midsized manufacturer of carpeting and floor tiles. Ray Anderson, the company's CEO and chairman, relates that Paul Hawken's book *The Ecology of Commerce* had a strong impact on him. The book takes on the issue of ecological destruction wrought by industrial activity. Anderson decided that Interface had a moral responsibility to transform itself into an ecologically sustainable operation. It redesigned its factories and production processes and worked with Cargill/Dow to substitute vegetable-based materials for those made from petroleum. The company also developed objective measurements to track its progress. According to Anderson, "We do it by measuring the total amount of stuff extracted from the earth, including by all our suppliers and including the energy we use, in order to produce a dollar's worth of revenue." The result, Anderson says, has been a decrease from 1.59 pounds per dollar to 1.21 pounds per dollar over the past five years.

This sort of positive effect was not the motivation behind Interface's choices, but without a doubt the focus on being good stewards of the environment was also good for business. Customers began to choose Interface over its competitors because of their shared environmental concerns. The decision has had even more far-reaching consequences—competitors have been forced by their customers to adopt similar environmental reforms, or else lose their business.[26]

In addition to such anecdotal evidence, doing the right thing from a global, environmental perspective has been objectively proven to be good for business. A recent study, sponsored in part by the University of Michigan, analyzed the stock-market performance of eighty-nine major U.S. mining and manufacturing companies that had production facilities in developing countries. The study found that those companies that implemented strict global environmental standards had a market valuation 80 percent higher (relative to the market value of their physical assets) than companies that used the less stringent local standards for their operations. In discussing why Wall Street valued companies with high global standards, the authors of the study noted that profits and growth may be hurt over the long run by such factors as bad publicity and the failure to anticipate changes in local standards. Setting a high standard builds employee morale and allows new technology to be diffused rapidly throughout an organization's international operations. Bernard Yeung, one of the study's authors, noted that "companies attracted by weak local environmental regulations may find that their short-run gain brings long-term pain."[27]

Do the Right Thing by Using Vision Acts

We take many actions—small and large, good and bad, daily and occasional—that play a role in shaping an organizational culture. Lorraine Monroe, founder and executive director of the School Leadership Academy in New York, says, "If you say you're about something, then what activities in your company indicate the reality behind those words?"[28] Monroe calls such actions "vision acts," and these acts can define an organization both internally and externally.

To be considered a vision act, an action must be motivated by a desire to do what is morally and ethically right. I'll begin with an example of a leader who intuitively knew he was supposed to do the right thing, but did not have the right reason. I was a young lawyer at a downtown Chicago law firm. The firm's managing partner was unfortunately more concerned with the firm's short-term bottom line than with instilling a core set of values to further the firm's mission. One day he called another associate and me into his office. Because the two of us had recently spent a lot of time wining and dining some of the firm's clients, the managing partner offered the following advice. "There will come a time when you are out with clients and, after everyone has had a few drinks, the question will come up, 'Do you want to go get a prostitute?'" My associate and I glanced at one another in disbelief. He continued: "Now, I don't want to tell you what to do. But, remember this: If you decide to go get that hooker, you will probably have fun, and the client will call you up the next day and laugh about the good time he had the night before. But he will never send you the 'big' case."

This directive fell short of being a vision act. Our boss was not concerned with the morality of hiring a prostitute; he was advising us merely to appear to act ethically so that we would get the big case. Both the other associate and I ended up leaving the firm shortly thereafter, in part because of the conflict between our personal ethics and those of the top leadership. This partner failed to understand that the firm could only realize its full potential by developing a culture that valued real integrity, not just the appearance of integrity. (As an aside, this law firm later disbanded due to lack of revenue-producing clients. Apparently, making a show of integrity wasn't even enough to sustain business! You can fool people for a while, but not for the long term.)

Christ-based vision acts, on the other hand, can have a positive impact on an organization, as the next two examples demonstrate.

Earlier in his career, John Mackovic, head football coach for the University of Arizona, had the top coaching position at the University of Illinois. There he inherited a program whose team had a reputation for occasionally playing "outside the rules." Mackovic refused to accept or condone this organizational culture. During his initial spring practice with the team, he talked again and again about the importance of the integrity of the game—how players and staff should conduct themselves both on and off the field—and made it clear that he would not tolerate disregard for the rules. Early in its first season, the team had yet to be tested. During the second quarter in a game against the University of Wisconsin, the Badgers were driving the ball deep into Illinois territory. Twice, on consecutive plays, an Illinois player committed a personal foul in an effort to hurt an opposing player. Mackovic quickly called time out, brought the entire team together, and told them in no uncertain terms, "We, as a team and as individuals, are better than this, and this is not who we are. We are a team of integrity, and we need to respect ourselves before others will respect us." The defensive unit went back out on the field and cleanly stopped the Wisconsin offensive drive in its tracks, and Illinois eventually won the game. Those associated with Illinois football credit Mackovic's rallying speech as the vision act that led to the creation of a culture that lifted up integrity as the cornerstone of its athletic program.[29]

At a recent President's Course offered by the American Management Association, I met an individual who had been hired a couple of years earlier as president of a plant that manufactured large machinery. When he was hired, the plant was financially on the ropes. Two months later he was asked to come down to the assembly line to make a decision. The foreman told him that the welding on a twenty-four-foot, $50,000 trailer was not properly lined up. The foreman said they had two options: The first was to re-weld and paint over the mistake so that the customer would not notice; the second was to leave it, since it did not make a real difference in the final outcome, and, again, hope it would go unnoticed. The new president said there was a third option, and asked for a blowtorch. He fired it up in front of all of the employees and proceeded to cut the trailer in two. The astonished foreman exclaimed, "Now what do we do?" The president replied, "Throw this one on the trash heap and start over!"

The president told me he went back to his office feeling very uneasy because he knew his company could not afford the cost of the wasted materials and labor. Nonetheless, he performed this vision act because he knew that, in the long run, the company would succeed only if it made quality the number-one priority. In the process of driving home his point, the president completely destroyed $50,000 worth of merchandise. But this "cultural story" has been passed down ever since to every new employee. The president finished the story by saying that he has never had another problem with quality at the plant. The lesson we can draw from this is that it pays—professionally and personally—to create our own vision acts and cultural stories.

Not every situation is quite that dramatic. The opportunity to create a vision act might be as mundane as correcting a supplier's invoice that mistakenly undercharges us. It is the consistency of our actions, however, that is important. As stated in chapter 2, when it comes to servant leadership, we cannot fake it. In creating a cultural story, we must back the story up with our actions, and this requires a consistent pattern of living and of interaction with fellow employees. It requires sharing the credit whenever possible, remembering that no task is beneath us, letting grudges and personality differences go, not gloating when we are right, not gossiping, and not being afraid to admit when we do not know the answer. In other words, it means acting with integrity and following the golden rule.

Do the Right Thing for Your Customers

As Christians, it is natural for us to want to improve the quality of lives of our fellow human beings. Once again, following the golden rule by taking care of our customers also makes good business sense. One of the most frustrating experiences in today's fast-paced world is buying an airline ticket. On most airlines, the price for the same seat, flying to the same destination on the same day, can range from $149 to $1,199. Airline policies that force an overnight stay on Saturday, or that require a purchase three weeks in advance, are made arbitrarily. Do you have a lot of frequent flier miles? Don't even think about using them for popular destinations during peak seasons.

One airline does things differently. Southwest Airlines has developed an organizational culture in which employees love their customers. The company talks openly about how their values do not allow them to implement policies designed to gouge their customers. Unlike other airlines, Southwest offers only three fares for each flight, usually between the $99 and $225 each way. The company also makes it easy for the customer to determine what fares will cost. Simply call, or go to their Web site, and see if seats are available for your flight in any of the three listed fares. The information is fully disclosed to the customer. If you fly enough to earn a free ticket from them, you can redeem it on any flight you choose, with the exception of five publicly identified blackout days each year. If there is an open seat in any price category for that flight, it's yours.

How has Southwest fared? It was the only airline in tragedy-plagued 2001 to make a profit and not lay off employees. Southwest truly understands that customer satisfaction, loyalty, and shareholder returns go hand in hand. Stephen Burnett, professor of marketing at the Kellogg School at Northwestern University, said it best: "If you run a company by the bottom line, you tend to not have a big bottom line."[30] While Southwest does not phrase it this way, its mission day-in and day-out is to do the right thing, and treat customers according to the Golden Rule of Leadership.

Every organization is in business to serve its customers. There is, however, no shortage of examples of companies that forgot about doing the right thing for customers and employees. AT&T is paying dearly for not keeping its eye on the importance of customer satisfaction. AT&T's business unit had more than six million customers and, in 1999, provided nearly half the company's revenue and more than half of its profits. In 1999 and 2000, however, AT&T attempted to improve the bottom line and increase shareholder value by cutting costs and letting go thousands of its customer-service representatives. Clients consequently were unable to get representatives on the phone, and it often took months to obtain service. Growth stalled, and other big interests, like PepsiCo, the U.S. Government, and Paper Mart reduced or completely severed their business relationship with AT&T. Telecom consultant Terry Smith said, "Virtually everyone that I deal with is either dumping AT&T or asking me to look for alternatives. I can't think of anyone that I deal with who wants to give them more business."[31]

How did the shareholders fare? In February 1999, AT&T's stock price was $63. By August, it had dropped to $29. By June 2002 it hovered around $10 a share. Contrast this approach to that expressed in a statement made by Scott McNealy, president and CEO of Sun MicroSystems in an interview on CNBC in April 2001—at the height of the high-tech downturn: "Our employees are our business. We are going to do everything we can not to lay off employees, even if it means a lower net profit for 2001." While Sun has certainly suffered during the economic downturn, the company remains rightly focused on the long term.

Another group of companies that didn't "get it" were the get-rich-quick Internet startups that focused on stock market valuation at the expense of providing long-term, genuine value to the customer. Companies like Dr.Koop.Com, Garden.Com, and Pets.Com lacked the long-term game plan, patience, and resources to build a healthy culture and competitive business model. In their eagerness to perform quickly, they left a multitude of burned investors, laid-off employees, and dissatisfied customers in their wake. While the founders of those companies may have had good intentions, and may have made money off of the initial public stock offering, few were around long enough to leave a lasting legacy. These shortsighted companies lost their investors' money, wreaked havoc in their employees' lives, did not serve their customers well, and added little value to society.

Netpliance, based in Austin, Texas, is another example of this misguided strategy. It developed and manufactured a simple computer designed only to access the Internet and send and receive E-mail. The company went public in 1999, raising more than $144 million and, at one point, had a market value of more than $1 billion. By 2001, its stock was selling for pennies a share. Netpliance had stopped providing promised customer support, leaving thousands of unsatisfied customers and thousands of investors who lost money. One former employee said about the company's treatment of its customers, "It just makes you feel rotten. . . . It almost felt like we turned our back on our customers."[32]

Compare this experience to a statement made by William R. Hewlett, cofounder of Hewlett-Packard:

> As I look back on my life's work, I'm probably most proud of having helped to create a company that by virtue of its values, practices, and success has had a tremendous impact on the way companies are managed around the world. And I'm particularly proud that I'm leaving behind an ongoing organization that can live on as a role model long after I'm gone.[33]

Do the Right Thing in Developing a Professional Career

I firmly believe that, as important as it is to "do the right thing" within our organizations, it is equally important to do the right thing in making decisions about one's professional career. The same Christian values that apply to all other aspects of our daily lives also apply to this arena. Earlier, I raised the issue of deciding whether to stay in a position at which one has been only a few months, or go with an offer from another organization that offered a substantial salary increase and attractive stock options. That was the situation in the Silicon Valley in the late 1990s. Employees referred to their current job as MTBOO—"Meantime, Between Other Offers." This attitude, it is important to note, wrongly assumes that how much money you make is the key factor in determining who you are as an individual.

In this era marked by the influence of Madison Avenue marketing campaigns, media fascination with the rich and famous, and endless cocktail party conversations about portfolios, it is easy to fall into the trap of assuming that money is the yardstick by which we are measured. Despite our cultural obsession with material wealth, however, money does not determine happiness. Historian Arnold Toynbee, in his *Study of History*, says that every major religion in the world agrees on what is important in life.

> These religious founders [Jesus, Buddha, Lao Tse, Saint Francis of Assisi] disagreed with each other in their pictures of what is the nature of the universe, the nature of spiritual life, the nature of ultimate spiritual reality. But they all agreed in their ethical precepts. They all agreed that the pursuit of material wealth is a wrong aim. . . . They all spoke in favor of unselfishness and of love for other people as the key to happiness and to success in human affairs.[34]

It can be a critical mistake for a person first to decide how much money she wants to make, and then find a job or career to meet that monetary goal. The result of that wrongheaded approach is to live with a lack of purpose and to miss opportunities to make a difference in the world. The important questions should be: What is my passion? What is it that I truly love to do? What makes me want to get up in the morning? Richard Kessler, former chair and CEO of Days Inn of America, puts it well: "If you focus on the money, you have eliminated the possibility of significance."[35] By pursuing our passion, we pursue significance.

Three different times in my professional life I have chosen another job or career that paid substantially less than what I had been making. On several other occasions, I turned down opportunities that would have paid significantly more. What framework did I use to make these decisions? My wife, Laurie, and I centered our discussions around the following questions:

1. What do I have a passion for doing?
2. What impact will a change have on our family?

3. Have I finished creating value in my current position?
4. Where is God calling us?

There are times when the answers to these questions seem contradictory. For example, during my eight years at Lutheran Social
Services of the South (LSS), there are periods of time in which it is
difficult consistently to maintain an intense passion for my job.
While I love our mission and the staff I work with, the extensive
travel can have a negative impact on my family and my health.
However, I also know that my calling continues to be at LSS
because I am not finished creating value within the organization.

After many discussions with my wife, and through much
prayer, it became clear that God's calling to me is twofold—to
continue my ministry at LSS for the short term, and to walk
through the doors God is opening up that are leading toward my
next career. God is providing me with appropriate professional
contacts and a long-awaited sabbatical to fulfill my dream of taking my learnings on leadership to a wider audience. God is opening up doors for new opportunities through the various boards I
serve on. God provided Laurie and me with a degree of financial
security so that, if necessary, I can accept less pay in my next position without adversely affecting our family. It also is clear that my
next calling is not going to be handed to me on a silver platter. I
need to take the initiative in preparing for a change in calling
while still fulfilling the demands of my current position. There
are times when balancing the two is not easy, and I am tempted
to give up. In retrospect, however, I realize that God continues to
answer my prayers, albeit in God's time frame, and not without a
good deal of hard work on my part.

Each person's "calling" in their life's work is unique; it means
different things to different people. Not all of us are called to emulate Mother Teresa and take a vow of poverty. I have a friend who,
while growing up, was completely taken with McDonalds—its
food, business, and marketing campaigns. His goal in law school
was to work in their corporate legal department. He reached his

goal and has achieved great professional success and personal satisfaction because he is an integral part of a company he truly believes in. From his perspective, McDonalds adds value by providing a quality product and by training hundreds of thousands of young employees—including many from disadvantaged communities—to succeed in the workplace. Throughout his career, he has made an impact on his colleagues, family, community, and church. Would he have been as successful working for another company, like Kmart? My guess is that he would not. His passion for the mission of that organization would fall far short.

I grew up in a family whose members had a long history of choosing church work professions. When I was in college, a friend of my parents asked me if I was going to follow in the footsteps of my father and work for the church. I answered that I planned to become a corporate attorney. I will always remember his response: "There is a real need for Christian business people. Never forget that this is a significant calling."

For the Christian, all of life means full-time service to Christ. That is true in secular and nonsecular careers. No matter what we do for a living, we are called to make a difference through our organizations, in our decisions, and in our interaction with others. Through prayer, hard work, and following our hearts, we will be given opportunities to make a difference by serving others. I pray that we all take advantage, every day, of the many opportunities God places before us in the high calling of our daily work.

chapter four

values-based
strategic planning

If I had eight hours to chop down a tree, I'd spend six sharpening my ax.
—Abraham Lincoln

Purposeful strategic planning
provides Christian leaders with an opportunity to instill Christ-based values throughout organizations, as well as be good stewards of the resources that God has entrusted to us. Blanchard, Hybels, and Hodges, in *Leadership by the Book: Tools to Transform Your Workplace*, discuss two aspects of leadership—doing the right thing (vision) and doing things right (implementation). They describe the vision of an organization as a "picture of the future that produces passion." Vision, which culminates in a clear strategic plan, has four main parts:

1. purpose: telling ourselves what business we're in
2. image: providing a picture of what things would be like if everything were running as planned
3. values: determining how we should behave when working on the purpose
4. goals: focusing our energy right now[1]

We who lead with faith have an advantage in setting a vision; we find it natural to infuse our organization with a clear sense of purpose and meaning. Our role as Christian leaders is to create and lift up our organization's core values and connect the values to the vision. We also have a responsibility to ensure that these values translate easily and can be effectively put into action by others. Finally, we have a responsibility to produce an end result that reflects that vision to customers and key stakeholders.

Strategic planning that is not done correctly reminds me of a cartoon depicting Moses coming down the mountain with the two tablets. The people exclaim, "Not another strategic plan!" How many of us have worked at organizations where, out of nowhere, the CEO pulls out a strategic plan and expects the staff to implement it? And, how often, after it has been paraded before the board and distributed at the annual senior managers meeting, does it go back in the drawer, where it remains until the following year?

Even worse are organizations in which the leader puts employees through the paces of a seemingly inclusive strategic planning process, but through manipulation, fear tactics, selective listening, and a top-down organizational culture "persuades" the other members of the strategic planning team to adopt his preconceived vision. What results is a dysfunctional, inefficient organization of uninspired followers whose focus is on their next paycheck as opposed to accomplishing the organization's mission. For strategic planning to achieve its purpose, the leader must be willing to accept that he is merely one of many voices in the process—a reality that is incredibly difficult but necessary to accept if the result is to be the creation and maintenance of a healthy culture and implementation of a vibrant strategic plan.

Richard T. Pascale, coauthor of *Surfing the Edge of Chaos: The Laws of Nature and the New Laws of Business*, captures the essence of this "old-game" planning strategy, in which a leader outlines what he feels is the best course of action, and then sits back to measure the results and tweak where necessary. Pascale notes that this old way of doing business no longer works; it creates organizations that stifle diversity and creativity and are less capable of change. It is necessary, now, to ask: "Has the environment changed so that I'm wedded to a former winning strategy that won't win in the new world?"[2] Planning that is initiated and implemented correctly results in key managers who have meaningful input into the plan; staff, customers, and stakeholders who know the plan and understand it; and staff who feel connected to the plan, and who understand their particular role in accomplishing its goals.

The Process

There are many methods of engaging in a strategic-planning process. The right process for a given organization is the one that demands a hard look at the organization's core challenges. Each organization will have different core challenges. Such challenges could include the need to adapt to new technology, changes in consumer preferences, new competition, an inefficient business model, decreasing profitability, a mature business cycle, and the need for more innovative products, to name a few.

The following is a general outline of a strategic planning process I have found successful in that it allowed our leaders to discover our shared values and impart them to every aspect of our organization. My preference is to use an outside consultant for part, if not most, of the process, especially when new members of the leadership team are interacting for the first time. Hiring a consultant has many benefits and brings several key elements to the process:

- a wealth of knowledge as the result of having gone through the process with other organizations
- rigor and objectivity
- freeing up the top leader to be an equal participant—not a facilitator and peacemaker

I have found using an organizational psychologist helpful as well, since an organization is basically a community of people who have voluntarily chosen to work together to accomplish common goals. The interaction between team members is often the most crucial aspect of successful strategic planning and implementation.

Leaders today sometimes tend to ignore the history of their organization as they look to the future. In order to devise a forward-looking plan, however, it is vital to understand where you have come from. Including such a "history lesson" in the planning process is time well spent, providing participants with knowledge of original corporate charters and bylaws, historical documents, photographs from the early days, memoirs of former leaders, and anything else that might give the participants a sense of the organization's original goals and purpose. It is often useful to engage in a dialogue about where an organization has or has not held true to its original mission, its values, and how it has adapted to changing environments. Such a historical review can move leaders to restore an organization's original values, or provide the courage to make needed changes in the face of an ever-changing environment.

Another vital component of the planning process is to gather and disseminate to the team relevant information about the organization in order to give a clear snapshot of the current state of affairs. I define as "relevant" any information that provides insight into the organization's current condition, such as data that demonstrates current trends vis-à-vis an organization's historical performance within its industry. Five-year comparisons often bring to light surprising trends that are vital to understanding an organization's current health.

Depending on the type of organization, relevant information might include:
- the true cost and net profit or loss for each of our services
- profitability charts broken down by customers, products, or geographical region
- competitor data and bench-marking analysis
- customer and stakeholder satisfaction and recognition surveys
- cost of capital data
- easily understandable financial information
- revenue growth charts reflected over a period of time

- market analysis information
- employee satisfaction surveys

When sufficient information is not readily available, ask whether the data is necessary to the planning process. If it is, then make an effort to collect it. Lack of sufficient available data can reveal much about the level of business acumen present in particular departments.

Next, take a close look at the mission statement. This enables everyone connected to the organization to determine whether its culture and values align. If the current mission statement does not convey a sense of power, change it. For-profit organizations are beginning to understand what many nonprofits have known for a long time—a compelling mission statement has a lasting impact on organizational culture. It draws the connection between the bottom line of an income statement and the "bottom line" of changing people's lives. It is how your employees and the rest of the world understand what the organization is all about. The Red Cross, for example, puts forth its mission statement in one succinct, powerful, easily understood phrase: "To Serve the Most Vulnerable."

After setting the mission statement, it must be *used* in order to prove effective. Display it in offices. Print it on letterhead and business cards. Include it as part of the process of interviewing prospective employees. Make it a key element of the first day on the job with new hires. It should permeate everything the organization does, including the act of strategic planning. Some organizations also choose to adopt a vision statement, which is essentially a more detailed description of the mission statement. This, too, must be clear, understandable, and compelling.

Next to be placed on the table are core values. An organization will not fulfill its potential unless it is mission focused and has values that are understood and "owned" by its members. If they have not already done so, leaders should take time to articulate, disseminate, and encourage adoption of its values. This is the time to engage employees at all levels of the organization. Leaders need to recognize that the employee who cleans the bedpans in a hospital may very well have the clearest sense of the organization's values, and would welcome the opportunity to talk about them.

Understanding the mission and the values of an organization are the two most important aspects of strategic planning. Organizational consultant Lynn Walker says that a strategic planning process fails often because employees see it as a required exercise, as opposed to an opportunity for them to create a belief system. He states, "In order for a strategic planning process to be successful, it must be an extension of an organization's belief system. And, for an organization to understand its belief system, it must first understand its values."[3] While the wording may occasionally change, the core mission and values of an organization should never change. They define an organization's identity and what it is about.

Strategy flows from values. As Roy Disney once said, "It's not hard to make decisions when you know what your values are."[4] Still, planning at this level is not without its challenges. The leadership team needs to be grounded in a clear sense of the key components of the organization—its current internal and external environment, mission, and values. Leadership needs to remain focused on developing a strategic plan—it is much safer, and therefore tempting, for groups to talk about operations rather than strategy. Strategizing opens the entire organization to introspection, which can be intimidating to participants. All organizations are perfectly designed to achieve the results they are getting. Whether or not a leadership team can change to achieve different outcomes is an open question, and a challenge that can be off-putting for some leaders. Personality conflicts and dysfunctional behavior among the leadership team can also prevent creative thinking and effective follow-through. True organizational change begins by looking within and being open to the possibility of changing how we see ourselves, our working relationships, and the world in which we operate. This is easier said than done. As Machiavelli stated,

"There is nothing more difficult for success, nor more dangerous to handle, than to initiate a new order of things."[5]

The core planning group should consist of the organization's top leaders. By the end of the four- to twelve-month process, all senior managers, as well as the board and key stakeholders, should have participated in some aspect of the process. In my organization of twelve hundred employees, approximately fifty senior managers, twenty-five board members, and forty key stakeholders had input at some point. In addition, senior managers were encouraged to involve their staff in aspects of the planning process. Managing such a diverse and large group can become unwieldy, but the process provides an avenue by which each member can feel valued and included as a key part of your organization. In a healthy organizational culture, mutual trust and respect will allow ideas to percolate from all areas of the organization. One way to give employees, at all levels, input into the process is to have the CEO or other leaders hold roundtable lunchtime discussions in an environment in which ideas and opinions can be shared honestly and without consequences.

The planning team should inform the governing board throughout the process and offer the board the opportunity to provide input at relevant points along the way. The board is also responsible for ensuring that the final product stays true to the organization's mission and values. It is the responsibility of management and staff, however, to initiate the planning process, make the final decisions in terms of strategy, and be responsible for its implementation. It is staff, after all, who best understand the internal and external dynamics that have an impact on the plan. Keeping this demarcation clear allows the board to hold management accountable, for it is management—and not the board—who "own" the plan.

Throughout, planners will need to give honest answers to the following questions:

- What new demands will we face?
- Who will be our customers, and what will be different about them in the future?

- What do our customers value?
- What do we need to do before anything else can happen?
- What are the two or three environmental factors that we worry about most?
- What are our strengths, weaknesses, opportunities, and perceived threats?
- What are we currently doing that we are very good at?
- What are we currently doing that we are not very good at?
- Which of our core competencies could translate readily into developing new opportunities?
- Do we segment our "better" customers, or do we treat all customers the same?
- What are we realistically capable of doing?
- What potential new business opportunities should we explore that fit within our culture?
- How well will what we are doing today resonate in the markets of the future?
- What is our unique market niche?
- What new competencies must be developed ahead of the changing environment?
- What is the talent level of our current staff and what is our capacity for innovation?
- How does the Internet fit into our short- and long-term plans?
- How do changing governmental and legislative agendas, sociodemographic changes, and new technology alter our way of doing business?
- How do we best allocate our financial resources?
- Does our current management have the capability to perform at the next level?

Answering the Mega-Questions

To ensure long-term viability and significance, every organization must also answer what I call its "mega-questions." The exact nature of the mega-questions will depend on the type of organization. For example, during his years at General Electric, legendary CEO Jack Welch relied on Peter Drucker to help him focus on asking the right questions. One such mega-question dominated Welch's management philosophy and actions: "If you weren't already in this business, would you choose to get into it now?" Answering this question spurred Welch to shed businesses in which he could not project that GE would be among the top two competitors. He focused, instead, on the businesses in which GE had achieved that level of success. This strategy—and the question that drove it—led to an amazing increase in GE's market value from $12 billion in 1981 to $492 billion in 1999.[6]

There are as many potential answers to Drucker's mega-question as there are organizations that choose to answer it. Gary Hamel, chairman of Strategos, believes that all senior management teams must ask themselves the following mega-question: "Are we building a legacy, or living off a legacy?" Organizations do well because past leaders had the foresight to formulate critical competencies on which legacies are built. Hamel points out that it is easy to attribute success to current leadership even when it is the result of past strategies and innovations. To make his observation concrete, he notes, "If Bill Gates cannot see beyond the PC paradigm, he will be the destruction of Microsoft."[7] In other words, even a giant like Microsoft cannot live off the legacy of its early days for an unlimited amount of time. Recently, senior management and the board of directors of Aid Association for Lutherans and Lutheran Brotherhood answered Hamel's mega-question by merging their organizations—with combined assets of $57 billion—to create Thrivent Financial for Lutherans. In this way they will harness their joint resources to build a new shared legacy that will better serve their constituency for generations to come.

If an organization is growing only incrementally in the same tried-and-tested ways of doing business, or if it is making money but losing market share, it is probably living off someone else's legacy. The question becomes: What should your organization be doing in order to guarantee that it will create its own legacy and add value to society, in keeping with the parable of the talents? Answering Hamel's mega-question allows an organization to challenge the status quo. It also challenges team members and leaders to ask, "What is the future of our organization if we don't do anything different over the next five years?"

Answering mega-questions such as those raised by Drucker and Hamel can be especially helpful in creating strategic plans in the midst of significant business and societal changes. For example, the concept of "planned abandonment" has surfaced recently in much of the strategic planning I've been involved in. This is the notion that what works today (or yesterday) may have little relevance for the future. Organizations that are capable of accommodating their way of doing business to the changing environment, and that can do it faster than the competition, have a huge competitive advantage.

Let me share with you one example of an organization that truly understands the concept of planned abandonment. Sheila Wellington ran a state mental hospital in Bridgeport, Connecticut, in the early 1980s. During her tenure, the facility endured a state-mandated budget freeze, was continually short-staffed, and was responsible for providing care to thousands of patients without having a say about how many or who they were. Faced with the dilemma of not being able to continue to do "business as usual," and not having the option of shutting the facility down, Wellington and her team decided to change the ways things were done. Among other things, they decided to

> train people who didn't have advanced degrees to act as case-workers. We forged partnerships with local family-care homes to provide extra beds. And we launched a day-treatment program, because we didn't have enough staff to run the wards all night. In the end, several of our solutions allowed for better care than the ways of the good old days. Today, programs like

day-hospitals are standard in community mental-health centers nationwide.[8]

Wellington and her team took advantage of a bad situation to reinvent the organization to make it a win-win situation for their clients and for the bottom line. Whether they actually used mega-questions in their discernment is not known to me. They had a clear view of the big picture, however, and understood that abandoning the past in order to create the future was creating a legacy that would benefit their organization and their clients.

Another mega-question that many organizations face is, "As we move forward, whom do we want to specifically target as our customers?" Implicit in this question are two more: "Which of our customers are we capable of serving best?" and "From which customers do we actually make a profit?" Examining the data and answering these questions led an Austin-based insurance brokerage firm to focus its marketing efforts exclusively on securing new clients with yearly revenues in excess of $1 million. They found that while they were good at serving smaller clients, their cost structure was such that profits from this category of business were minimal at best, and long-term viability required cultivating customers whose purchases provided better margins. Most organizations serve a variety of clients, including "lower-end customers"—those who do not use your product or service as much or as often as customers who provide you with more profit, or who cost more to service than other subsets of customers. An organization like Merrill Lynch or Bank of America might define a lower-end customer as someone who has less than $100,000 in assets invested in their products. A hospital might define him as one who visits its emergency room and does not have health insurance. It is a mistake to try to fit the needs of both higher- and lower-end customers into the same model, or to ignore one or the other group completely. The airline industry understands the need to differentiate its services to meet the unique needs of its customers. They have been particularly successful at differentiating customer types using the concept of frequent flier miles and by creating various levels of preferred customers based on how much they fly each year. Charles Schwab also tailors its levels of service to customers based on how much money each customer has invested.

As we intentionally plan for our future, these and many other examples lead us to ask: "Is it in the strategic interest of our organization to create alternative business models for each category of customers?" For example, it may make financial sense for a hospital to open a clinic in a community where demographics indicate that a large percentage of residents have no insurance. Doing so could allow the hospital to access other government-based revenue streams, create wellness programs to reduce the number of trips to the emergency room, provide education about preventive medicine to reduce the overall cost of treatment, and allow a hospital to achieve its mission of providing healthcare to every member of the community. Willingness to create new models and take well-planned risks can create alternative business models that are win-win solutions for your customers and your organization.

There will be times when an organization will simply be unable to continue providing gold-plated service to lower-end customers. A planning team needs to consider the opportunity cost of no longer differentiating among customers when it comes to service provided. How your team deals with that issue opens the door for providing services that are tailored to customers' unique needs. In other words, creating alternative business models to fit customer needs is another way to implement the Golden Rule of Leadership.

Create the Plan

After reviewing the internal and external data and having an honest dialogue with board members, senior managers, and stakeholders, your leadership team should be ready to create several alternative paths of action that are achievable. One possible path is to continue living off past successes, fine-tuning them for use over the next five years. Another may be to shed programs or products that no longer make sense for the future of the organization, and focus instead on expanding its core competencies. Yet another might be to seek partners, alliances, or a merger if it no longer makes sense for the organization to "go it alone." After creating these various paths of opportunity, it is up to the leadership team to decide the best path or paths to follow. In a healthy organization, the right decisions are often obvious, but not always easy. The team will create a path that does not necessarily force change on the organization, but rather discovers leverage points that will create healthy, long-lasting change.

The next step is to communicate, communicate, communicate! Do so verbally and in writing. This is a primary responsibility of the CEO and, in my opinion, one that can be shared but never delegated. The reality is that all relevant audiences—employees, stakeholders, customers, and board members—need to be told repeatedly what the mission is, what the values are, and what the plan of action is. To accomplish this, make use of all forms of communication. Information about the strategic plan is shared most effectively when the "top" executive relays it personally, in writing, E-mail, newsletter articles, posted signs, and conversations. Effective use of a variety of communication methods ensures that the message will be heard and that employees will understand its importance. But that is not always the case. The CEO of a board I sit on shared the organization's new vision at a recent board meeting. It was the third time he had done so. At a subsequent board meeting, however, a member raised her hand, and said, "We really need to have a vision." She, and others on the board, had certainly "heard" the message, but it had not been communicated in a way that made it their own. John Kotter, Harvard Business School professor, says that communication must be easily understood. He encourages the use of metaphors, analogies, and examples, stating that in order to be effective, a message must be relayed in multiple forms. The

CEO, he says, must lead by example and be ready to explain any seeming inconsistencies.[9]

Execute the Plan

Once a plan is in place, the real work begins. A strategic plan is only as good as the process used to implement it. The planning team has taken the important first steps by identifying a common set of beliefs about the organization's purpose and mission, answered key questions, explored various paths of opportunity, and made important decisions. It is vital at this point for senior management to make an unwavering commitment to follow through with the plan, or else all of the hard work will have been for naught. It is wise to execute the plan with eyes wide open to the fact that, no matter how inclusive it may be, there will be pockets of resistance, simply because change is hard and people's turf is threatened. A CEO must apply all of his personal leadership skills for the plan to become a "living" document. Gordon Eubanks, president and CEO of Oblix Inc., a software company, succinctly states, "Strategy gets you on the playing field, but execution pays the bills."[10]

Under the management philosophy I have outlined, execution includes creating action plans at the departmental level that are linked to the strategic plan, job descriptions that are linked to the action plans, and performance appraisals that are linked to the job descriptions. Personal development plans should be created for key staff members to acquire new skills. And leadership should prepare a comprehensive summary of the action plans, and disseminate it throughout in order to track the degree to which it is being followed.

Throughout this process, the leadership team needs to ask itself the following questions:

- Do we have the right organizational structure and the necessary talent to accomplish the plan?
- Have we properly linked the plan to our operational and capital budgets?
- Is our culture aligned to our strategy?

- What information, training, and resources do our key managers need in order to accomplish their piece of the plan?
- Have we fully developed our action plans and set up a system of monitoring and assessment?
- Are our employees performing as expected?

All activity in the organization must be linked to, or in service of, the strategic plan. Toward this end, the team needs to recognize the difference in how leadership and management "see" the organization: leaders look ahead one, three, five, or ten years; managers look to the next day, or month, or year. A process for each needs to be developed in order to maximize the potential of both.

Once the strategy is in place, it is important that the organization avoid being distracted by chasing opportunities that are not part of the overall strategy. It may be tempting to jump at a business venture or opportunity that looks too good to pass up. The best first step, however, is to take a step back and determine if it fits with the overall strategy. Bear in mind that, as a living document, the strategic plan is subject to change as more information becomes available and new opportunities arise. It may, in fact, be a wise decision to adjust the plan midcourse in order to accommodate such changes. Reassess the plan systematically and according to an arranged schedule, asking and answering questions such as these:

- What external and internal factors have changed that will impact the plan?
- What has worked and what has not?
- Were certain aspects of the plan more like a "field of dreams" where, just because we built it, we expected customers to come?
- What midcourse adjustments do we need to make?

A truly effective planning team recognizes that no strategic plan is perfect, and is able to adjust the plan to accommodate unforeseen changes.

Assuming a New Leadership Situation

In too many situations, those who step into a leadership role—from outside an organization or via promotion—find themselves in an organization that is unfocused and adrift. I have already alluded to the fact that this is often the fault, not of the organization itself, but of a previous leader who failed to recognize when it was time to leave, or who was forced out. In both instances, the previous leader leaves behind a "ghost" that can make itself known in the low energy level and general indifference of employees. The opposite scenario, of a leader having the foresight to leave at the right time, is all too rare. Two examples of this type of transition at the top took place recently at General Electric and Southwest Airlines, when radical changes in leadership caused barely a hiccup. These companies had a proper transition plan in place so that everyone, including the new CEO, clearly understood and embraced the organization's vision and core values.

There are several things that the leader, whether newly arrived or already in place, of an adrift organization can do to help it regain its moorings. First, the leader must remain calm and confident. If the leader is not, no one else will be, either. Next, she needs to get the existing management team focused on who the customers are and who the competitors are. This gives everyone a unifying vision during what could be a difficult time. Eubanks emphasizes how a good beginning is vital to executing a plan successfully. He forces his organization to get focused with this charge: "Of all the possible battlefields, let's figure out where we have the best chance of winning, and why we feel that way. Then let's move in that direction."[11]

As a starting point, it is useful to ask members of the leadership team two questions: "What are three things that I need to do in order for the organization to succeed?" and "What are three things that you need to do in order for the organization to succeed?" Their answers will provide a wealth of information. They will allow the leader to gauge the motivation and energy levels of the leadership team members, as well as their creativity and ability to think outside the box. The answers will also provide insight into starting points for creating some easy, early wins that will motivate and rally the troops, as well as instill confidence in their leader. And, during those initial months while ratcheting up the level of activity, it is vital to begin a new strategic planning process. When Lucent Technologies was spun off from AT&T in 1995, CEO Henry Schacht devoted the first six months of his time creating a shared strategy and culture among his top fourteen executives. He believed, correctly, that it was vital that all of his top managers believe in and work from the same script in order for their spin-off to succeed.[12]

Nonprofit and For-Profit Organizations Can Learn from One Another

One of the painful outcomes of strategic planning is that decisions for the long-term good of the organization often involve short-term pain. It is my experience that nonprofit organizations have a harder time making the sacrifices necessary for the long term than do their counterparts in the for-profit sector. The latter are often light-years ahead in terms of developing both short- and long-term strategies that create value. Their leaders are often better trained and better disciplined, having had to function under the unforgiving rigor of the market. Nonprofit organizations have not had the benefit of responding to relentless market pressure, and often have historical or cultural limitations that limit their potential leadership pool.

The church denomination I belong to still insists that ordained clergy lead many of its auxiliary organizations, some of which have multimillion dollar budgets and hundreds of employees. These pastors often have little or no management experience. Similarly, many universities continue to look to academicians to lead their large and diverse institutions. These former professors may be brilliant, but probably have little experience in fundraising, strategic planning, or leading a large organization. The board of an organization must act in situations like these to make sure its leader receives the proper management training. The new leader must also have access to appropriate consultants and be provided with a leadership coach. All these initiatives need to be properly budgeted for at the front end, and made nonnegotiable items during the budgetary process.

For years, many nonprofit institutions and their donors have allowed inefficient and ineffective organizations to exist and even receive financial support. This is no longer the case. Donors, customers, regulators, and lending institutions today are demanding the same kind of fiscal discipline from nonprofits that institutional investors have always demanded from for-profit organizations. They are, in fact, playing the role that the market has historically played in keeping for-profits efficient and nimble. They are requiring answers to questions that have never before been asked. How does your organization objectively measure success? Does your financial situation support your strategic plan and organizational structure? What standards of measurement do you use to show that your organization is truly making a difference? These questions, and their answers, have tremendous implications for those who serve on the boards of nonprofit, university, government, or religious-based institutions. The leader of a nonprofit is not only expected to perform at a higher level, but also to demonstrate that good intentions translate into results, and to provide objective data to support those results. The bar has been raised. The simple fact is that nonprofits who are unwilling to borrow and implement ideas from the corporate world will not be around for the long term.

There are many nonprofit organizations with leaders who recognize this. These nonprofits, as a result, are far ahead of for-profits in terms of creating vision and aligning their corporate culture to support their vision and belief systems. Organizations like the Salvation Army, MedStar Health, the Red Cross, and Valparaiso University have been outstanding at creating a vision and developing communities that empower staff, volunteers, and stakeholders to work together—often at great personal sacrifice—to accomplish shared goals. Many have been so successful that the more enlightened for-profit organizations are looking to them for insight to help them run their own organizations more effectively. For example, many Fortune 500 companies are having their managers read *The Most Effective Organization in the U.S.: Leadership Secrets of the Salvation Army.*[13] It might come as a surprise that the Salvation Army is described by Peter Drucker as "the most effective organization in the world."

I believe strongly that truly visionary organizations in both sectors are nearly identical in purpose and structure. For example, there is little difference in terms of organizational structure and values between Johnson & Johnson and MedStar Health, a non-profit organization that operates eight hospitals as well as other healthcare facilities in Maryland and Washington, D.C. A well-run for-profit organization often looks and feels like a well-run nonprofit organization. And a well-run nonprofit organization will want to be judged by for-profit standards. There is much to gain by adopting the natural strengths of each model. Christian leaders have an advantage in both the for-profit and nonprofit worlds because our biblically based values provide us with the framework to implement our prayerful and difficult decisions in a compassionate and heartfelt manner. We also lead with the confidence expressed in 2 Chronicles 20:15: "Do not be afraid. . . . For the battle is not yours, but God's."

What Do the Experts Say?

Like life itself, strategic planning is a continuous learning process. I have been fortunate in my career to have as mentors two values-oriented, Christian experts in strategic planning—Lynn Walker, a St. Louis-based organizational consultant, and Dick Tesauro, an organizational consultant from Dallas. I feel every executive can benefit from his or her own "coach," whom they can trust and go to for advice. I have also gone through a number of strategic planning processes that have helped shape my thinking. There are several other key resources I have found helpful, and which I recommend to anyone on a leadership journey.

Good to Great,[14] by Jim Collins, has been adopted as our organization's other Bible during our 2002–2003 strategic planning process. Two findings from Collins's trail-blazing research on how a good organization can become a great organization has had a tremendous influence on our discussions, planning, and actions. First, as demonstrated by Collins, an organization must have the right people on the bus before it determines where it is going. Contrary to popular belief, it is imperative to have the right leaders in place prior to engaging in strategic planning. Take the time to determine if the right people are on the team. If not, go out and get the right people and put them on the organizational bus. It is only at this point that an organization can effectively determine and execute its strategy. Second, in what Collins refers to as the Hedgehog Concept, every organization must answer the following three questions:

1. What are you deeply passionate about?
2. What drives your economic engine?
3. What can you be the best in the world at?

In order for an organization to become truly great, it must develop the rigor to focus exclusively in the areas where the above answers overlap. A strategic plan must revolve around what the leaders and organization are passionate about, what provides an appropriate margin, and what the organization is truly world class at executing and delivering.

Another resource that has helped clarify my thought process is Collins and Porras's *Built to Last: Successful Habits of Visionary Companies*. In it, the authors describe the difference between being merely an organization with a vision statement and being a truly visionary organization in which culture and vision are aligned. They state:

The essence of a visionary company comes in the translation of its core ideology and its own unique drive for progress into the very fabric of the organization—goals, strategies, tactics, policies, processes, cultural practices, management behaviors, building layouts, pay systems, accounting systems, job design—into *everything* that the company does. A visionary company creates a total environment that envelops employees, bombarding them with a set of signals so consistent and mutually reinforcing that it's virtually impossible to misunderstand the company's ideology and ambitions.[15]

If an organization is aligned, this should be readily apparent to all who come in contact with it. Values define an organization and differentiate it from others. Staff, customers, and stakeholders should be able to infer the values of a well-aligned organization without having to see them in print. And, while it is crucial that an organization's core values never change, its strategies, structure, systems, and policies should always be open to change.[16]

Another useful concept we have adopted from Collins and Porras is the idea of creating a Big Hairy Audacious Goal (BHAG). A BHAG engages people. "[It] reaches out and grabs them in the gut. It is tangible, energizing, highly focused. People 'get it' right away; it takes little or no explanation."[17] Examples of BHAGs are former President John F. Kennedy's pronouncement that "We are going to the moon." Or GE's goal "to become number one or number two in every market we serve." Similarly, WalMart, in 1990, set a BHAG to double the number of stores and increase sales volume per square foot by 60 percent in ten years. And it did.

The organization that I lead has also used the BHAG concept successfully. Six years ago we created an internal goal of becoming the largest and best provider of children's services in the state of Texas. At the time, we were at best a minuscule player. Four years later, with a lot of hard work and a few sleepless nights, we accomplished our goal and currently provide more than $30 million in services to children in the state. In

2000, we created a BHAG to raise more than $5 million from our donors for our programs. This was significant in that we had raised just over $3 million in our most successful year up to that point. We stated our goal publicly, put our plan in place, and tracked it on a monthly basis. When we accomplished our BHAG, we took the time to celebrate our success properly. While some doubted whether we could attain our goal, we knew we were capable. As Collins and Porras note, BHAGs look "more audacious to *outsiders* than to insiders."[18]

To create change that is sustainable and that adds permanent value is difficult in any organization. One of a leader's most important roles is to make the case for change and then create an environment that allows change to occur. One book that has been instrumental in how I view this topic is John Kotter's *Leading Change*. Kotter describes why, in most organizations, new strategies aren't implemented well, acquisitions do not achieve expected synergies, reengineering takes too long and costs too much, downsizing does not get costs under control, and quality programs do not deliver hoped-for results.[19] As a remedy, Kotter outlines an eight-step program to produce meaningful, lasting change.

1. Establish a sense of urgency
2. Create the guiding coalition
3. Develop a vision and strategy
4. Communicate the change vision
5. Empower employees for broad-based action
6. Generate short-term wins
7. Consolidate gains and produce more change
8. Anchor new approaches in the culture[20]

Kotter's program is useful because it not only provides a game plan, it also accurately describes the pitfalls that can occur along the way. For example, he asserts that for significant change to occur, a large percentage of employees must go far beyond the call of duty in their daily efforts. In an organization of one hundred employees, "at least two dozen must go far beyond the normal call of duty to produce a significant change." In an organization of one hundred thousand employees, the number might be as high as fifteen thousand.[21] Leaders can make this happen by creating a sense of urgency and by properly communicating it to others.

The last resource I will offer enabled me to conceptualize an organization in terms of its natural life cycle. The life cycle of every organization can be symbolized by the S-shaped Sigmoid Curves depicted below:

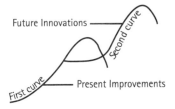

Like a roller-coaster ride, organizations often grow at a steady pace, everyone enjoying the ride to the top. But products mature, they become commodities, leaders get complacent, the market changes, and the ride down can be dramatic and steep. Ken Blanchard and Terry Waghorn, in their instructive book *Mission Possible: Becoming a World-Class Organization While There's Still Time*, describe how an effective organization should not only pay attention to where it is positioned on its *present* curve, but should simultaneously begin creating its *future* curve. They describe as world-class an "organization that is working effectively, not just on one curve or the other, but on both at the same time, and learning from both."[22] By simultaneously paying attention to both curves, your organization will be able to adapt to external changes before a crisis has developed.[23]

This visual has helped me understand that some of the daily activities in our organization are devoted to maintaining and improving the curve we are currently on, while other daily activities are devoted to creating our future curve. Using this concept has helped us decide, for instance, whether we need to add employees in order to create the second curve. I categorize all my leaders as first curve, second curve, or combination leaders. I am much more forgiving of mistakes and revenue shortfalls as the result of actions taken by second-curve leaders. They are blazing new ground as they create the second curve.

Let's Get Busy!

The role of a leader is to manage the broad brushstrokes of the entire strategic-planning process. In today's world, a leader who gets caught up in the details will fail, with the end result being a lack of shared ownership and, ultimately, short-lived follow-through. It's a near guarantee that the strategic plan will end up a dead document collecting dust in employees' desk drawers. At the same time, a leader in today's fast-changing environment does not have the luxury of developing a bottom-up decision-making process marked by painstaking research that requires scrutinizing all the data before "pulling the trigger." In the end, however, a leader can steer the process so that it is dynamic, variable, and Christ-based, and help shape the organization's core values based on the Golden Rule of Leadership. In that spirit, the organization will achieve its full potential by creating an environment that allows employees to make decisions, to take risks, to make changes, and accomplish mission-driven goals.

Virtually everyone in an organization wants the freedom and opportunity to make decisions, in their realm of responsibility, that further the mission of the organization. By leading under the tenets of the Golden Rule of Leadership, we as leaders are in a position to give our employees this opportunity. This is not only the appropriate Christian response, it also once again makes good business sense. We have moved, in the twenty-first century, from a command-and-control leadership model to a shape-and-influence model, from a hierarchical organizational chart to one that reflects a network of colleagues. James Copeland, CEO of Deloitte Touche Tohmatsu, holds that the difference between the two models is not just a distinction between the "new economy" and the "old economy." Instead, he separates the eventual winners and losers by distinguishing between companies "that are able to incorporate change, to reinvent themselves, to take advantage of technological improvements, and those that can't." In talking about an effective strategic planning process, Copeland states:

> What you can do is control the plan, the broad strokes of what you're trying to get done, and be sure that the planning process is dynamic and variable. Control the culture of the organization—the critical shared values, the things you don't want to change, that you want to anchor the organization with in periods of big change—and then let people in that environment be empowered to do things, to make things happen and take risks. When your people do things really well, it reflects well on you. When they do things that turn out to be mistakes, you have to be willing to stand up and say, "It's my responsibility." If you can accept that, you can operate in this environment.[24]

True leadership is not a matter of position. It is the person who thinks conceptually who is a leader. One measure of a leader's job performance, with respect to strategic planning, is the number of additional leaders that have been created in the organization. A planning process that is inclusive allows for the creation of leaders and attracts and retains high-quality people who prefer to work in a culture in which they have the freedom to lead. The end result will be a good strategic plan that gives the organization a solid framework for success, one that will allow senior managers to create their own plans, make their own mistakes, and create their own destiny. A leader can enable the process by providing new leaders with mentors and teachers from the leadership team to create an environment that encourages creativity and forgives mistakes. A leader who is willing to make the effort, and willing to spread the responsibility of leadership throughout the entire organization, will continue to add value to the organization in today's changing environment.

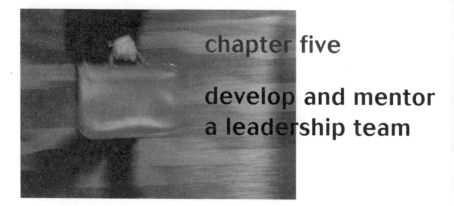

chapter five

develop and mentor a leadership team

Leaders don't create followers, they create more leaders.
—Tom Peters

Developing and mentoring a leadership team is as vital a task as choosing those who serve on it. A strategic planning team will not function on automatic pilot. Its members, regardless of background, creativity, and talent, need encouragement and direction. And as they benefit from being mentored, they, too, will want to develop and mentor their own teams of employees. This process is yet another way in which following the Golden Rule of Leadership adds long-term value to an organization.

The Gospel of Matthew demonstrates that Jesus created not followers, but leaders, as he chose, developed, and mentored his team. Glen Kehrein walks us through the process: Jesus first handpicked his leaders (Matt. 4:18-22). He did so with intention, aware of the importance of selecting those with whom he would surround himself and who would be his team working to spread the gospel of salvation to the world (Matt. 28:19-20). Jesus took time to teach his disciples the values and principles of his ministry in such settings as the Sermon on the Mount (Matt. 5–7). From among his chosen twelve, Jesus selected three—Peter,

James, and John—and spent extra time with this "inner circle," recognizing their extra potential and empowering them for ministry. Finally, Jesus was a servant to his disciples, even stooping to the humble task of washing their feet (Matt. 20:26-28).[1] Jesus serves as a model for implementing the Golden Rule of Leadership in the important task of empowering a team to achieve its goal.

We often view our children as being our legacy. As Christian leaders, we might also think of our employees in the same light. What better legacy to leave than colleagues who will some day be in a position to make a significant difference in the world? It is very gratifying to see others grow and mature due in part to one's influence and example. It is even more of a blessing to know that the role we play in helping others develop reflects responsible stewardship of our God-given talents. As Charles Handy has written in *The Age of Paradox*:

> True fulfillment is, I believe, vicarious. We get our deepest satisfaction from the fulfillment and growth and happiness of others. It takes time, often a lifetime, to realize this. Parents know it well, as do teachers, great managers, and all who care for the downtrodden and unfortunate.[2]

Blanchard, Hybels, and Hodges say that when servant leaders combine "loving care" with a proactive commitment to grow and develop those they lead, the result is a special kind of leader.[3] Noel Tichy, in *The Leadership Engine*,[4] describes how the best organizations are those that are filled with people who reproduce leaders who reproduce leaders. If members of the leadership team act upon a sincere passion to develop and mentor their respective teams, it will become natural for their subordinates to emulate their actions. This practice will soon affect every position and person on the organizational chart. In this chapter, we will explore why developing and mentoring leaders is vital to the success of an organization.

Once Again, It Is Not Your Father's World

In today's professional world, the terms of the once-revered unspoken employment contract have changed. Companies can no longer guarantee employees a long-term future because the future is more uncertain than ever and organizational needs change in response to a number of uncontrollable factors. As leaders of enlightened organizations operating in today's environment, we promise to provide employees with challenging work and to help them grow as individuals. As products of a culture shaped by expectations of immediate gratification and a strong drive for self-improvement, workers today promise to give their best effort only if the organization keeps those promises. The reality, however, is that no matter how well you treat today's up-and-coming employee, he will always keep his options open. His ultimate loyalty is not to his employer, but to himself. This is especially true for the newest generation to enter the workforce.

Members of generation X have been raised reading the cartoon *Dilbert*. They see in him the reflection of their parents, who put their loyalty and trust into their place of employment, only to be downsized, rightsized, or abandoned by the organization. These young workers rightfully understand that true job security comes from sharpening their skills and being self-reliant. As a result, younger workers will stay with an organization as long as they believe that they are valued and challenged and are continually improving their skills. Managers who fail to pay attention to their needs will quickly lose talented people. These up-and-comers will also keep established leaders on their toes—today's employees simply will not tolerate bad managers. Donna Kindl, senior vice president of human resources for Monsanto, predicts that in "five years, bad managers won't exist. People don't have to work for lousy managers who don't understand their needs. Companies can't afford [bad managers]."[5]

What the Research Says

Being a good manager and developer of people is a role God asks us to undertake. In Philippians 2:3-4, Paul writes, "In humility consider others better than yourselves. Each of you should look not only to your own interests, but also to the interests of others." Following these instructions can also benefit your organization. A recent Gallup poll found that 19 percent of employees were "actively disengaged" from their work. Some reasons given included the sense that they were unsure of what was expected of them, they did not have the right resources, they did not have any friends at work, and they felt their bosses ignored them. The study also found that disengaged workers missed more days of work and were less loyal to their place of employment. Gallup estimates that this "disengagement" costs American organizations an estimated $292 billion to $355 billion a year. Gallup found that a primary variable in determining whether employees were "engaged" in their work is the manager to whom they report.[6] Similarly, Charles Schwab found that the number-one cause for turnover was poor manager performance.[7]

What is it that employees really want from their employers and supervisors? A study conducted by the Hay Group surveyed 500,000 employees in more than 300 companies over a three-year period and found three key factors that influenced the decision to stay or not to stay with a company. First, employees crave the opportunity to learn new skills. Second, they want to receive coaching and feedback from their supervisor. The third determinant was the nature of their work.[8] Yet another research project had similar findings: the *1998 Human Resource Financial Report* reported that the number-one reason employees leave their jobs is their perception that employers offered limited opportunity for personal development and advancement.[9] And a Towers Perrin survey uncovered three main criteria that contribute to an employee's perception of the performance of his or her supervisor:

1. My supervisor deals fairly with everyone—does not play favorites

2. My supervisor motivates me to do my best
3. My supervisor effectively helps me understand how I can grow and develop within the company[10]

Such research highlights what today's employee expects of an organization. Money is certainly an important factor. Even more important, however, is the opportunity to grow, to work with people who are interesting and who treat you fairly, and to have a supervisor who is a mentor and not a traditional "boss." Managers, of course, are in a position to respond to these expectations by applying the Golden Rule of Leadership to manager/employee relationships. When managers exceed employee expectations, the result will be more effective workers and a positive impact on the long-term success of the organization.

The Interview Process

Managers have the responsibility to find the right person for the job, retain that person, and maximize that person's performance. The supervisory role begins at the time of the interview process. It is a cliché that a leader should hire people smarter than herself. Taken to the extreme, this would make the janitor the most intelligent employee in the organization (which is, not surprisingly, sometimes the case). But the dictum is basically sound. I look for three things during the hiring process. First, I want an individual whose core values are as strong or stronger than mine. This gives me an employee I can trust, and who will be a role model for me and others. Second, I look for someone who is smarter than I am in his or her area of expertise. This person can teach me new things and can become a team leader by putting together a solid strategy and operational plan. Third, I look for someone who can be a team player—someone who models effectively the role of a servant-leader.

Hiring an individual who satisfies these qualifications is only the beginning. Next, the individual must, ideally, be retained for the long run. This task, too, begins during the interview. At an initial interview, a manager has a unique opportunity to explore a candidate's long-term goals and to begin creating a plan to help achieve them. A plan for one person might mean to arrange for her to take courses in Web design or corporate finance. For another a plan might entail gearing the current job toward an eventual promotion by building the acquisition of broadened skills and experience into the job description. Team members have a right to expect that they will continue to grow throughout their careers. The leader's role is to help them fulfill their dreams so that they and the organization will benefit now and in the future.

Implementing an Effective Management System

To manage employees successfully is not rocket science, and the most effective management practices are easy to implement. However, due to sloppy practice, inattentiveness, and just plain laziness, many organizations fail to follow a few simple rules that I consider "the basics" of employee management:

1. create a comprehensive job description for each employee
2. create individual yearly objectives for each employee
3. meet with each of your reports on a regular basis to review the job description and objectives, determine if modifications need to be made or if the employee needs additional resources and/or assistance, and have a frank and constructive conversation about his or her performance
4. hold each employee accountable for accomplishing specific goals
5. measure and monitor both individual and group performance on a year-to-year comparison basis
6. communicate regularly about both positive and negative developments in the organization
7. develop and facilitate opportunities for employees to offer ideas and complaints
8. minimize perks based solely on job title

Implementing and adhering to these basic management principles is the first step toward motivating and enhancing employee performance, as well as creating an organizational culture characterized by fairness. From here, management is well positioned to go the extra mile in making a difference in employees' lives and adding value to the organization.

Connect Employees to the Organization's Mission

Not every employee has the luxury of interacting with clients on a daily basis. Members of the accounts payable team, for example, may rarely come face-to-face with a client during their daily routine. This lack of interpersonal contact makes it hard for many employees to remain deeply connected to the organization's mission.

It is a supervisor's responsibility to ensure that workers remain emotionally connected to the mission. Management can help accomplish this by putting the organization's mission and values into writing and then communicating them through every possible medium—town hall meetings, stories, employee newsletters, and videos.

An effective American Airlines television commercial shows a company mechanic walking through a busy terminal looking at the families waiting to board the plane. The faces remind him of his responsibility to do quality work when servicing an airplane by linking what he does for a living to the lives of real people. This commercial is designed, of course, to inspire consumer confidence in the airline's commitment to quality and safety. It is also a good example of how an organization can make the connection between the work of a single employee and its overall mission and values.

An accounts payable team in a hospital could be encouraged to walk through the halls and talk with patients, or be given time off to volunteer in the hospital. The method of connecting employees to the mission will vary according to the situation. The key is to provide as many opportunities as possible for employees to "touch" the mission. This will motivate them to do their best.

Reviewing an Employee's Performance

The yearly performance review, while necessary, is only a small part of what it means to provide an employee with effective feedback. Leigh Abrams, president and CEO of Drew Industries, tells the story a colleague related to him about a bright young employee who was leaving his organization. His friend called the employee into his office and asked him why he was leaving. The exchange went like this:

"I don't feel like I'm needed," the employee said.

"Just two months ago we gave you a big raise at Christmas and told you that you were doing a great job."

"Yeah, but that was two months ago."

"Well," the executive replied, "How often do you think we should tell you you're doing a good job?"

"Every day," the young employee said.[11]

This story is a reminder of how important it is to offer praise on a regular basis for a job well done, and of what a small part annual performance reviews play in meeting this responsibility. The key to effective praise of an employee's good performance is to do it often, make it specific, and, whenever possible, do it publicly.

Instant and daily feedback is vital in today's world in order to retain and motivate employees. But it is just as vital for employees to offer honest feedback on manager performance. One way to establish the trust that is needed between managers and their reports is to encourage solution-focused feedback. For example, let's say that you, as manager, and an employee have been working together on an account, and you have just finished presenting a proposal to a client. Following the meeting, you might ask your coworker for an honest critique of your pitch. Ask for specific examples of what you could have done differently in order to improve your performance, always keeping the critique focused on content, not on personality. This prevents the conversation from becoming "open season" on you, and focuses instead on specific, positive suggestions on ways you can improve your skills. Making yourself vulnerable in this way can deepen the level of trust between supervisor and employee.

The Need to Be Honest and Direct

Adhering to the golden rule dictates that we as Christians have a responsibility to be direct and honest. Look at the values statements or personnel handbooks of most organizations today and you will find verbiage about treating employees with fairness and respect. This sounds good on paper, but is often difficult to carry out. It means, among other things, a commitment on the part of supervisors to share with employees topics that are not always pleasant. It requires that, if necessary, we tell an employee he is not doing his job or that his talents simply do not match his position. It is not easy to tell people what they do not want to hear. We would prefer to be courteous, or even to remain silent, rather than speak the truth and risk hurting someone's feelings. By refraining from being honest, however, we do a disservice to both the employee and to the organization. Those who work for us deserve to be treated with honesty and directness. I have found that employees desire to be held accountable for their work, and want constructive feedback on how they can improve their performance.

And, of course, there are times when an employee is not performing up to expectation. When that proves to be the case, the first step I take, as a leader, is to evaluate my own role in this perceived "failure." I ask myself these questions:

- Have I clearly articulated my expectations of him?
- Has she had enough training and does she possess the right tools and information to succeed in her position?
- Am I being a faithful mentor, or am I leaving him on his own too much?

- Am I adequately empowering her to do her job?
- What other external factors are preventing him from accomplishing his tasks?

Only after answering these questions to my satisfaction will I sit down and have an honest and direct conversation with the employee.

There is no one-size-fits-all approach when it comes to confronting an employee about performance failure. The message must be tailored to the situation and the personality. For example, if he thinks along logical lines, then relate to him in a logical manner, staying away from abstractions or appeals based on passion. The only constant rules are:

- communicate in private, never in front of anyone else
- discuss the situation immediately after it has occurred or has been brought to your attention (I once had a supervisor who made notes of his employees' wrongdoings, put them in their file, and went over them one by one at their annual evaluations; this is not a good method)
- communicate in a caring way that demonstrates a motivation not to judge, but to help them improve
- above all, be honest and direct

It is also important to be sensitive to any signals of personal or family issues that may be causing a loss of focus at work. If this is the case, a manager should relate this concern, explore how to be of help, and offer to allow some time (within limits) for him to work on his personal issues, find the support he needs, and get refocused on work.

It simply is not fair to let a below-average employee continue to under-perform. It is the duty of a Christian leader to give an honest assessment to each employee on a regular basis, help him obtain the necessary skills or motivation, and, if all else fails, ask him to leave. Following Christ's example, we seek the ultimate good of another; that will sometimes mean saying or doing things which, while painful at the time, will help him find his true calling. To fail at this Christian responsibility could harm the organization and, more importantly, could contribute to a cycle of repeated work failures on the part of the individual. This could have a devastating impact on him, his family, and his community.

It is paramount, then, to have frequent, productive conversations with employees about both good and bad performance issues. This reduces the stress of the yearly performance review and diminishes the chance of surprises. The Outback Steakhouse restaurant chain uses an interesting version of this concept. Managers use no form of written evaluation, but instead are expected to communicate with their staff face-to-face before and after every shift.[12] I have found that if my direct reports and I communicate honestly and directly on a regular basis over the course of the year, the annual performance review time becomes a natural, easy, productive dialogue between two trusting colleagues. We discuss our shared objectives for next year, how we can better help the other accomplish future goals, what training and development is needed to further enhance our skills, and what challenges we might undertake to further our organization's mission as well as push the limits of our professional capabilities.

The Use of Rating Systems

Many organizations have adopted rating systems with which to assess employee performance. In one such system, managers utilize either an individual or collaborative process to assign employees to various categories—say, the top 20 percent, the middle 60 percent, and the bottom 20 percent. General Electric, for example, requires its managers to rate each employee on a scale from one to five, and to encourage those with low ratings to look for positions in other organizations.[13] Another example comes from Metropolitan Life Insurance Co., which for years had a reputation of being bureaucratic and slow to respond to change. When Robert Benmosche took over as CEO, he developed a leadership program and an accountability process. The program is designed to teach the top 5 percent of its forty-one thousand employees how to be visionary, make good decisions, and establish their own mission that supports the MetLife vision. Benmosche's philosophy is that effort without results does not count. He instructs each management team to go through a collaborative and often difficult process to decide which employees are in the top 30 percent, which are in the middle 50 percent, and which are in the bottom 20 percent. It is Benmosche's belief that in order to compensate adequately and recognize the top 80 percent, it is necessary to identify the bottom 20 percent. This process has helped MetLife retain its best employees while prompting the less-productive ones to move on.[14]

Rating systems such as these have their place, and may work in specific situations, assuming the other pieces of good management such as a healthy culture, appropriate mentoring and evaluation programs, and adherence to following the golden rule are in place. Ratings systems can help managers identify and initiate honest discussions with low performers. ICI (Glidden) Paints found such a scoring system useful. Lee Nielsen, former vice president of Human Resources, commented: "The success was based on managers having frank discussions with employees about needed changes—especially with the bottom 20 percent. We found that after two or three conversations, which took place once a quarter, these employees either left on their own, improved their performance, were reassigned to a role they could perform, or were terminated. But we had a much higher percentage of employees voluntarily leaving than being terminated."[15]

As a caveat, rating systems are not an appropriate management tool for every organization or in every situation. For example, if not implemented fairly or with compassion, or implemented in an already unhealthy organizational culture, this type of review system has the potential to do great harm. It can create mistrust and be perceived as an inherently unfair means by which a manager can manipulate data to the advantage of his "favorites" or discriminate against older employees. In addition, the usefulness of such systems is limited when an entire team is performing at high levels. I would not want to be placed in the situation of ranking the vice presidents that make up my executive team. Because we currently have the right people on the bus, all are top performers and add value to our organization.

Ratings systems should be seen as merely one of many tools for management, and should not be relied on exclusively. No such system can ever be a substitute for building relationships with employees.

Letting Someone Go

No one enjoys having to let an employee go. Most try to avoid it like the plague. Some, especially managers in nonprofit organizations and churches, are apprehensive about firing an unproductive employee because they feel it is not the compassionate thing to do—that it is somehow not Christian. But by keeping unproductive employees on the payroll, these organizations end up enabling low performance, both individually and collectively.

Lynn Walker correctly observes that "too often being nice is thought of as synonymous with being a Christian."[16] Sometimes, trying to be nice actually harms the one you are trying to help. The point is that "niceness" can camouflage the truth, and then no one is served. Some managers justify inaction by blaming the tight job market, saying they would not be able to find a better replacement. But there is great cost involved in keeping an unproductive employee. Poor performers create demoralizing down-cycles that influence the entire organization by keeping other employees from reaching their potential, performing at half speed, or, ultimately, leaving to find a more stimulating work environment.

A Christian leader must be fair and results-oriented, but never paternalistic. She recognizes that her employees are human beings. In deciding whether or not to fire someone, a leader must first make a dispassionate, informed determination about what is best for the organization. She should ask, "Will it make a difference if the employee and I develop an action plan to help his performance?" And "Are there positions within the organization for which the employee is better qualified?" If the answers are no, even a Christian leader has a responsibility to humanely ask the employee to leave the organization.

An effective and compassionate way to handle this type of situation is to let the employee know privately that in a certain number of days you will have to terminate him. Share with him that because of your concern for him, you wanted to let him know now so that he could begin making other plans and voluntarily resign at any time during this period. Tell him that you trust him and expect him to continue to support the organization during this time period, and that if his actions do not concur with this mutual agreement, he will be terminated immediately. Depending on the situation, other compassionate Christian responses include paying for outplacement assistance and/or providing a generous severance package. As others hear about the decision regarding a fellow employee, they will come to know that you expect results from those who work for you, and that consequences will follow if they do not occur. They will also witness how compassionately and fairly you handled the situation, and they will respect you for this.

If a manager has been honest and direct all along with an employee who has been underperforming, the employee will, more often than not, choose to leave voluntarily. I once inherited a secretary who had been with us for a very long time, but had not kept up her computer skills and was quickly becoming a hindrance to the success of our organization. I told her that she needed to update her skills in order to keep her position, and offered to give her time off and to pay for the necessary computer course. A couple of days later, she came back and told me that she had been thinking about spending more time with her grandchildren and that she was ready to retire. We threw a big party for her, and she left happy, having made her own decision. I was honest and direct and compassionate toward her, and trusted her to do what was right for her and for the organization.

Employers sometimes fear letting someone go because they believe it will harm office morale. Actually, the opposite is more likely true. Those who are doing their job well do not want to be in the company of those who are incompetent or unproductive. From their perspective, firing a worker who is not doing his job is a matter of justice and equity. They understand that a colleague's substandard performance means increased work for them, and that it is keeping the organization from achieving its potential. By handling the matter in a Christian, humane fashion, management earns the respect of employees, and models for them what it means to go the extra mile for another.

A while ago, our organization was forced to deal with illegal drug use among two employees at one of our children's residential treatment facilities. We talked about instituting a random drug-testing program, but were afraid our employees would rebel over their perceived loss of privacy. We decided to bring the issue up at an employee meeting to get their feedback. To our surprise, they were overwhelmingly in favor of drug testing. We discovered that they felt having competent coworkers and achieving the mission of helping abused children was more important than their temporary loss of privacy.

Firing a worker is simply a responsible way of telling them that they are in the wrong job. It helps them understand that their current position simply is not their calling in life. It usually isn't anything more or anything less. Keeping someone who is incapable of doing his job is the same, in effect, as telling that individual a lie. When the time comes for firing someone, it can go "well." Other times, it does not. After some time passes, however, that person will more often than not feel thankful about the loss. The action forced him to reconsider his life—to make decisions about what he liked to do and did not like to do, what he was good at and was not good at, and where he could most effectively contribute his time and talents—and choose a direction that better suited himself and the world.

Using Compensation As a Management Tool

Compensation systems have a direct impact on employee motivation. Many compensation systems are overcomplicated and have little influence, if any, on employee performance. Some can even have an unintended negative impact. For example, many organizations base their incentive plans and salary increases on whether financial targets have been met. But in many cases, this has resulted in undue pressure to backdate sales invoices, overload distribution channels, and pay production workers overtime to ensure that the manufacture of a product is completed and shipped by quarter's end. Or, by using budget-based targets, organizations unwittingly enable their employees to set easily attainable targets. The result can be inefficient, self-serving, shortsighted actions that can reduce long-term value.

What is the solution? It is important for an organization to create a compensation system that truly reflects employee performance and that objectively measures whether he or she has added long-term value to the organization. During the past decade, some sophisticated organizations have used what is known as the "Balanced Scorecard" measurement. In addition to measuring traditional financial data to assess performance, this system uses other indices of performance that most clearly predict the outcome of an organization's long-term strategy. In a typical balanced scorecard system, relevant metrics from the following areas are measured:

- customer metrics: how customers view the organization
- business process metrics: how well the organization's core processes produce value
- internal development metrics: how well the organization learns and grows
- financial metrics: how well the company meets shareholder needs

Use of the balanced scorecard system signifies a renewed realization that undue emphasis on decisions designed to improve short-term financial results can inadvertently hurt the long-term value of the organization. If created and implemented properly, this system can help link an organization's compensation plan to its long-term strategy. For example, under this system, an executive's at-risk portion of his compensation can be tied not only to measurable financial results, but also to objective, measurable customer satisfaction metrics, employee satisfaction and retention metrics, and metrics related to being a good citizen of the community. This system is certainly not a substitute for creating the right organizational culture, but it has the potential to complement and be one of many tools in your strategic arsenal.[17]

Be a Mentor

Being a mentor is a fulfilling way to bring out the best in people, strengthen the organization, prepare for eventual transitions in leadership, and fulfill Jesus' mandate to serve others. Dr. Stephen Graves, cofounder of the consulting firm Cornerstone Group, lists in broad terms the goals of being a mentor:

- to transfer experience to those who are less experienced
- to help leaders become more mature
- to transfer vision
- to transmit values in a culture
- to pass along strategic information
- to offer a listening ear and helping hand with problems
- to effectively confront negative intentions or behaviors
- to motivate and encourage, or give "ego biscuits"
- to foster a sense of independence in the protégé so that he can make it on his own[18]

The mentoring process benefits both the mentor and the protégé. The mentor gains by watching another blend his values into everyday actions. The mentor learns by watching the protégé approach issues from a different framework—history, knowledge, and life experience—than the mentor's.

Mentoring can be done on a formal, scheduled basis, but I prefer to do it informally, incorporating it into my management style. Either approach can be effective and, to a certain extent, depends on the type of organization and the personality and work styles of both parties. The end result of successful mentoring is a healthy, collegial relationship that benefits the organization by achieving the following results:

- it builds loyalty and trust in the workplace
- it creates an intentional mechanism to grow leaders who will bridge the future and provide lines of succession
- it helps retain great people
- it provides a way to use hands-on, real-time training
- it offers a way to honor, maximize, and replace an aging workforce
- it opens up and improves relationship pathways[19]

Jim Hushagen, a partner at the Seattle-based law firm Eisenhower & Carlson, describes how serving as a mentor benefits him both tangibly and intangibly. His mentoring experience has resulted in clients being better served, increased profitability, and improved firm retention. It has also increased his enjoyment of the practice of law and fulfilled his desire to teach others how to add value to their client's lives.[20] It is yet another example of how following the Golden Rule of Leadership benefits all parties.

Over the years, I have been privileged to help those who work with me accomplish their dreams—some, by moving up the ladder within our own organization; others by becoming leaders of other organizations; and still others by preparing for their next career. A talented vice president who worked under me once confided to me his dream of becoming a consultant in his field. Some time later, an opportunity arose that allowed him to provide some limited consulting services to a couple of other organizations. I readily agreed to let him take a few days to pursue this lead. The few days he missed in the office were more than offset by his increased loyalty to our organization. The experience also enabled him to develop further his skill sets, which had obvious benefits for us. Will I some day lose him as an employee? Probably. But I am confident that, as a result of his positive experience with us, he is mentoring others within our ranks, and, when the time comes, will leave our organization stronger than when he came.

Stretching Employees to Greater Achievement

One important aspect of the mentoring process is to stretch the capabilities of the best employees. I have felt the most satisfied professionally when my mentors placed me in situations before I was ready—mentors like Dr. Les Bayer, who promoted me to assistant to the president of Concordia University at Austin after just two years in higher-education administration; Michael Whouley and John Dukakis, who gave me major responsibility on the campaign trail; and the Lutheran Social Service Board of Directors and Bob Greene, who named me CEO of a $30 million organization at the age of thirty-six. Looking back, I cannot say I was truly "ready" for any of these challenges and responsibilities. I did not have the experience that one would normally expect of a person in those positions. But my superiors had the confidence that, with the proper mentoring, I would rise to the occasion.

The excitement of a new challenge and the corresponding fear of failure got my adrenalin pumping like nothing I had ever experienced. I was passionate about doing well, and was not about to allow myself to fail and let my mentors down. My experience has taught me a valuable lesson about professional growth. If you really believe in an employee, if you feel he has the right attributes, and if you provide him with the proper support, then giving him more responsibility than he has a right to expect at this point in his career is good for him and for the organization. I suggest that leaders take a hard look at each of their subordinates and ask, "When is the last time they had an assignment or project that really made them stretch beyond their comfort zone?" If the answer is more than twelve months, it is possible that good employees may be starting to think about their next career move.

Pay Attention to Fairness Issues

Fairness in life matters. For Christians, fairness is at the heart of the golden rule. If we are serious about the golden rule, even getting in the grocery store express line with more than twelve items in our basket is out of the question. Fairness in organizational life matters, too. And, it is not just the final outcome that must be fair—employees care equally as much about the fairness of organizational processes. There are three aspects that characterize a fair process in organizational life:

1. engagement: involving individuals in decisions that affect them by asking for their input and allowing them to refute the merits of other ideas and assumptions

2. explanation: everyone involved and affected should understand why final decisions are made as they are

3. expectation clarity: once a decision is made, managers must state clearly the new rules of the game

These three are especially applicable when it comes to conducting performance reviews, determining salary increases, deciding who gets what perks, and ensuring that everyone receives an equal opportunity to interview for internal job openings. Research has proven that the more effectively a fair process can be incorporated into organizational decision making, the more likely employees are to trust management, accept outcomes that are not in their favor, and make short-term personal sacrifices to further the interests of the organization.[21]

Witnessing As Examples of Christ

I consider myself a Christian who is most comfortable witnessing to my faith by example. I am not one to hand out Bible tracts or publicly proclaim my faith to my colleagues. I tend to follow the admonition of Saint Francis of Assisi, who said, "Preach the Gospel always and when necessary use words." My goal is that others, observing how my values and belief system influence my personal and professional behavior, might see in me a little of Christ. I have occasionally been successful at accomplishing this goal. On any number of occasions, colleagues have initiated conversations about my Christian faith, which has given me welcomed opportunities to share with them what I believe. As servant-leaders, our witness to Christ in word and action has great potential for influencing those around us. I strive every day to be prepared at all times for the occasion to be a good witness, that others might encounter God when they interact with me.

In regard to Christian witness, the most important advice I can offer is that in developing relationships with employees, it is vital to simply be oneself and to be genuine in all interactions. And this returns us to the truth espoused earlier—the need to be authentic and to act without pretense or arrogance. Being authentic requires us to listen truly to others and treat them as the important people they are, regardless of their position. It comes from knowing and being open with others about our own limitations, and caring about meeting their needs. It comes from being honest and patient. It comes from being devoted to seeking the greatest good from others.[22]

How many opportunities do we have in life to leave a lasting legacy, improve the long-term value of our organization, make a difference in someone else's life, and serve as Christ's example? God lays this before us. I only encourage you to not waste it. Let me close this chapter by listing some of the divine insights God offers as we go about our daily business of developing and mentoring others:

"Be at peace with each other." (Mark 9:50)

"Be devoted to one another." (Romans 12:10)

"Instruct one another." (Romans 15:14)

"Greet one another." (Romans 16:16)

"Serve one another in love." (Galatians 5:13)

"Carry each other's burdens." (Galatians 6:2)

"Be kind and compassionate to one another." (Ephesians 4:2)

"Forgive each other." (Ephesians 4:32)

"Submit to one another out of reverence for Christ." (Ephesians 5:21)

"Teach and admonish one another with all wisdom." (Colossians 3:16)

"Encourage each other." (1 Thessalonians 4:18)

"Build each other up." (1 Thessalonians 5:11)

"Spur one another on toward love and good deeds." (Hebrews 10:24)

"Confess your sins to each other." (James 5:16)

"Pray for each other." (James 5:16)

"Clothe yourselves with humility toward one another." (1 Peter 5:5)[23]

chapter six

balancing family and professional life

The trouble with the rat race is that even if you win, you're still a rat.
—Lily Tomlin

It is essential for a true leader— and especially a Christian leader—to balance family and professional life. When we make a genuine effort to lead a life that reflects a healthy sense of priorities, we benefit not only ourselves and our families, but also our organization.

It naturally follows that a leader whose life is in balance will want to encourage the same sort of balance among employees. Research shows that people who lead balanced lives will be more productive in what they do for a living. But as we are all too aware, the delicate art of achieving balance is easier talked about than accomplished. This makes it incumbent upon leaders not only to set the example, but to implement programs that help employees lead balanced lives. By following the Golden Rule of Leadership, we show our commitment to our employees' best interests, and go a long way toward securing the long-term success of our organization.

Today's Christian business executive faces constant assaults against leading a balanced life. Modern technology, via laptops, cell phones, personal digital assistant devices, fax machines, beepers, and other "conveniences," has made it increasingly likely that we will take our work home—and on vacation, and to our children's school events, and so on. But the converse is also true. When we take care of personal business at the office—buy stock, plan vacations, attend to personal E-mail, surf the Internet—we essentially bring our home life to work. Given these realities, we are forced to accept the fact that home and work life do—and will continue to—collide. Some people, myself included, embrace this melding of the two worlds. In fact, more and more individuals are shunning the idea that work time and leisure time must occupy separate "space." A phrase has even been coined to describe this modern phenomenon: "virtual farming." In this paradigm—much like the romantic notion of the bygone family farm—results are what matter most. Life is to be viewed in its totality, like a meaningful work of art, and not merely in terms of what can be accomplished from nine to five at work, or, for that matter, from five to nine at home. As Paul instructs us, "Whatever you do, work at it with all your heart, as working for the Lord, not for men" (Col. 3:23).

Many have commented about the downside to the hyper-competitive nature of the new economy. Robert Drago, professor of labor studies at Pennsylvania State University, writes:

> Employees are being asked to handle work-family conflict by having their families fade into the background. Firms are providing services that allow workers to work harder and longer so their productivity will continue to rise. The downside is that people are spending less time dealing with family problems. They are giving up control over their family life and letting other people make their decisions.[1]

Former U.S. Labor Secretary Robert Reich has written eloquently about the bleakness of the new economy. In *The Future of Success*, he argues that the new economy causes people to lead more frenzied lives while having less economic security, which results in a corresponding loss of time and energy for family, community, and self. Reich documents how Americans are working longer hours and are more stressed than ever before. He demonstrates how, viewed solely from an economic perspective, "there is no good excuse not to work except for intervals when one has made a clear and principled decision not to, in order to do something else. However, the threshold for deciding to do something else keeps rising as work keeps getting more accessible."[2]

Ellen Galinsky, president of the Family and Work Institute, a New York-based organization that researches work patterns, describes the problem this way: "The way people work has made them end up with more pressured lives. Work creates the problem. Then work creates the solution, rather than dealing with the problem."[3] Elaborating on this cycle, she says, "Jobs affect home life three times more than your home life affects job performance. [This] causes a chain effect where the negative home life then affects job performance."[4] The actions and policies of an organization have a real impact on employees' personal lives. Christian leaders have the opportunity and responsibility to create an organizational culture that keeps the negative characteristics of the new economy to a minimum, increases employees' quality of life, and contributes to the long-term success of the organization.

To create that kind of effective culture at work, our own lives as leaders must have balance. Only then can we broaden our focus to those around us.

Create Your Own Priorities

As a business executive, I have established three life priorities—my faith, my career, and my family. Through some conscious decision making with my family, I am able to work sixty hours a week—including volunteer and community service—and still have plenty of time with my wife and daughter. There is no longer room in my life for such distractions as watching sporting events on television or playing recreational golf (except as family activities), nor for such time-consuming activities as mowing the lawn or trimming the trees. We have decided that paying others to perform these tasks is a good investment in our family's future. A sixty-hour workweek—plus fifty-six hours for sleep and twenty hours for jogging, showering, running errands, and other necessary activities—still leaves thirty-two hours for significant family time.

If we understand the importance of working to create a God-pleasing family unit, why is it so hard to accomplish? One reason is that the home and work environments are so vastly different. The dynamic of what goes on at work has the potential to engulf everything else in life. When we walk in the office door, we are met with daily, weekly, quarterly, and yearly deadlines, and the reality of reacting to business cycles. We are expected to produce specific outcomes during those various overlapping cycles, or we will be considered a failure. We feel, at least subconsciously, the pressure of those "behind" us who would love to have our job. It is when we are at work that we have the most energy, look our best, and are put on a pedestal for our skill and successes. Let's face it: the place we work can be a very gratifying, ego-building, seductive environment.

Contrast this with our life at home. We walk in the door tired and still consumed by the pressures and deadlines of work. The house is a mess. We rarely feel that our children place us on a pedestal. The Internet, cable television, telephone, unfinished work, and other distractions keep us from spending quality and quantity time with our loved ones. Unlike our time at work, there are no quantifiable outcomes by which our time at home is measured on a daily, weekly, quarterly, or yearly basis. Any "results" achieved in our home environment are less tangible; they are the "squishy," hard-to-measure outcomes like the quality of our family relationships or appreciation for community service.

But that does not make these outcomes any less significant in terms of the impact they have on our lives. Some very real negative outcomes can be associated with our physical and psychological absence from the home. The following facts drive home that point:

- in a home where the father is absent, a teenage girl is three times more likely to engage in sexual relations by the time she is fifteen years old
- teens in father-absent homes are at greater risk for illegal drug use
- children in father-absent homes have a higher rate of asthma, anxiety or depression, and behavioral problems[5]

While some of these outcomes may manifest as "delayed reactions" later in a child's life, they are ultimately far more devastating than failure to meet a work deadline or satisfy quarterly market expectations. By not placing as much focus and energy on our faith and our family as we do on our work, we can literally destroy the lives of those we love. I have worked with high-level politicians and have been professionally and personally associated with some of the most successful business leaders in our country, and have yet to find any job that is worth this high cost of forfeiting family relationships. For the person of faith—whether running a billion-dollar corporation, managing a department in a community hospital, or serving as a pastor—giving first priority to those loved ones, in whatever form the person's family takes, is not an option. It is a duty and responsibility.

Arlie Russell Hochschild, in her book, *The Time Bind*, talks about the "reversal model family" where "home is work and work is home." In her research of women in the workplace, Hochschild found that many women preferred to be at work rather than at home. Her data showed that these women felt more appreciated at work; developed their strongest friendships at work; found mentoring their subordinates to be more satisfying than parenting their children at home; and, in time of crisis, such as the death of a parent, their coworkers were more helpful than their family or church. Hochschild writes:

A tired parent flees a world of unresolved quarrels and unwashed laundry for the reliable orderliness, harmony, and managed cheer of work. . . . The more attached we are to the world of work, the more its deadlines, its cycles, its pauses and interruptions shape our lives and the more family time is forced to accommodate to the pressures of work.[6]

For a Christian leader, the question becomes, "How many work pressures can my family withstand before I compromise long-term outcomes at home?" It takes great discipline to be an effective leader and a great spouse and parent. It begins by having a vibrant relationship with Christ. This includes being involved in church, participating in regular Bible study and home devotions, and engaging in constant prayer. These take no special skill—only a willingness to develop these patterns of living.

It is also vital for family members to communicate honestly about their goals and expectations as individuals and as a family unit. Based on numerous conversations among our three family members, I have set the following personal and professional outcomes for myself:

- to achieve a long-lasting, vibrant marriage
- to raise a healthy, well-adjusted daughter who enjoys being with her family, is well educated, a strong Christian, and who, with our guidance, will discover her own personal path to serve others meaningfully
- to have a significant career in which I serve others

It is by conscious choice that I did not list, as one of my goals, to climb to the top of my field in the professional world. If this can occur without sacrificing my other goals, so be it. But I believe that by striving to achieve these three outcomes, I will have done my best to fulfill God's desire for me as a Christian.

How does this play out in the real world? My wife, daughter, and I have talked openly about concrete things that affect our family. For example, while we love living in Austin, Texas, we would gladly live elsewhere should the Lord call us to serve others in a different place. In addition, Laurie and Sydney also have helped me know the time parameters within which I can function to avoid placing an unhealthy stress on our family. Those parameters include a career that requires being away from home no more than two or three nights during the week, as long as I am present for dinner—physically and emotionally—the other evenings, and home on most weekends. What they rightfully veto are any job opportunities that would demand my being out of town for weeks at a time, or that would mean consistent late-night office hours. They also veto any job in which my heart is not in the mission, no matter how large the salary might be. They understand that the stress inherent in such a conflict simply would not be worth the extra money.

As a husband and father, I respect their wishes and support the decisions our family has made. There is no way I can fulfill my familial responsibilities if I am away from home and unavailable much of the time. And, quite frankly, I would not want to live that way. My daughter will be this age only once. I cannot imagine not sharing her experience of being a second-grader and all the joys and fears that time entails. All the corporate and organizational challenges I may be "passing up" will still be there when she is older. When George W. Bush won the 2000 presidential election, many colleagues and friends figured that, because of my connections to his campaign and because of my background, I would apply for a job with his administration. But I had no interest in pursuing such a career. I knew from past experience that the intensity, long hours, and all-consuming nature of working in Washington, D.C., would not be conducive to success in two of my three goals. My decision to stay where I was surprised others but was in keeping with my personal priorities.

Including family-oriented goals in my life's list of priorities does not mean that work takes a back seat. In reality, work still comes first on most days, as far as what occupies my mind and my time when I am not at home. Leading a multistate social-service organization with twelve hundred employees is time-consuming and stressful. Laurie and Sydney understand that the needs of

the thirty-six thousand clients we annually serve are also important. But they trust that I will be disciplined enough to give my
work the attention it needs and still achieve a balance between
work and home life. They also make it one of their family roles to
help me achieve my professional goals. This includes putting up
with out-of-town travel, attending organizational functions, and
responding to the occasional work emergency that might inter-
fere with some important family events—including, for example,
my daughter's kindergarten graduation ceremony.

Each person needs to develop his or her own path to maintaining a healthy life balance. Some have found mentors, life
coaches, or a personal board of directors useful. Others, like
myself, rely on their spouse as a trusted coach and advisor. For
me, maintaining a healthy balance is made easier when I perceive
my three—often-competing—priorities on equal footing. This
gives me the freedom to adjust my focus accordingly, depending
on the immediate needs of any given priority. As an accomplished
juggler (a skill honed during the many hours I spent on the bench
during my limited collegiate baseball career), I learned that I need
to be aware of all of the balls in the air while simultaneously
focusing on the one in my hand. As I write this paragraph, I can
hear Laurie and Sydney playing outside in the pool. But because
I have my "professional ball" in my hand right now, I am not feeling distracted by their play. Joining them would make for some
excellent family time, but there are other hours already built into
this day for that. Losing my focus on writing this chapter would
prevent me from accomplishing the professional objectives I have
set for myself today. The "family ball" will be falling into my hand
soon enough.

This is another way of saying that we should make the most
of every single minute at work. I actualize this rather vague concept by consciously treating every workday as though it were the
last day before vacation. Think about how much work you get
done when you are intent on clearing your desk and accomplishing your objectives so that you can enjoy that needed time off.

For those who find their work to be their calling, this practice can be developed with a little discipline and focus. As James Evans, CEO of the Best Western hotel chain puts it: "You don't have to be the one who works the most hours, just the one who is most there during the hours you work. Come to work and put your heart on the table."[7]

It seems almost paradoxical that the more time we take off from work to reconnect with family or with oneself, the more productive and effective we will be as leaders. A great periodical, *Life @ Work: Blending Biblical Wisdom and Business Excellence*, devoted an entire issue to this topic, under the title "Understanding the Biblical Mandate to Rest."[8] The authors point out that if we do not work, we are, in fact, lazy, and cannot fulfill our calling. Yet if we do not rest, we are indeed shallow and unable to assess our direction in life and to worship God. Elsewhere, noted author Jeremy Rifkin talks about how a person's creativity is developed through intimate relationships and deep play.[9] The strength of our relationships with others, and the freedom to find time to "do nothing" and engage in "deep play" is dependent upon our ability to see the future creatively, to imagine how to better serve our customers, and to how we can develop processes that will make our organization more efficient.

I have taken to heart advice offered by Stephen Covey. In *First Things First*,[10] Covey says we can choose to live either by a clock or by a compass. If we live by a clock, we are consumed by appointments, objectives, schedules, and activities. If, instead, we choose to live by a compass, we are guided by our vision, values, principles, mission, direction, and destiny. By staying true to our compass, we can shape our life so that what is truly important to us remains central. In other words, we need to know when to say yes and when to say no. We need to focus on and give 110 percent to our compass, and learn to say no to anything that will upset our life's balance. The words Laurie loves to hear most when I come home from work are, "I said no again today." She knows exactly what saying no takes, and is thankful for my recently acquired ability to say it.

Some colleagues have told me they would burn out if they were to focus exclusively on the two realms of family and work. They find it important for their own life balance to take time away to go hunting or play golf in order to sustain themselves over the long haul. Laurie and I have found that, for us, it helps to look at our life together in stages. Each stage is a distinct chapter. In our first stage—newlywed and childless—we had plenty of time for our careers, as well as time to play golf, see friends regularly, and watch television. Now, in our second stage, as parents responsible for the rearing of a child, we recognize that those things must temporarily be put on hold. We also recognize that they will again be a part of our lives when our daughter becomes more independent in her teenage and college years. Then we will begin the third chapter of our life, when choices and priorities will change yet again. The decisions we make in the current stage of our life are not binding forever. Rather, this is a time when we acknowledge what is most important to us right now as we work toward accomplishing our twin goals of having both a meaningful career and a God-pleasing family life.

Helping Employees Balance Their Lives

In addition to paying attention to the need for balance in our own lives, as leaders we must also pay close attention to the balance—or lack of balance—in the lives of those around us at work. A leader is the role model in working to achieve an organizational culture that reflects a healthy personal-professional balance among employees. That means going beyond the call of duty and burning the midnight oil when the situation dictates. It means volunteering to cover an out-of-town meeting so a colleague can go to his son's baseball game. It means letting employees see that it is okay to take the morning off to attend your daughter's class field trip, or to leave at a reasonable hour in order to be home for dinner. By this behavior, a leader demonstrates that family can take priority while still getting work done effectively. The leader earns the respect of the members of the organization, who will likely emulate these values in their own lives.

It is no secret that an organization will not profit when employees are burned out; quality of work will suffer, productivity will decrease, and employees will be less loyal and more likely to leave. In an ideal organizational culture, employees will voluntarily work hard during crunch times or in times of crisis or opportunity. But when work demands are not as urgent, they will also take time to nurture their personal lives. The more freedom employees have to lead balanced lives, the more satisfying their personal lives will be; this, in turn, pays dividends in the quality of their performance at work.

What the Research Says

Helping employees balance their lives by following the golden rule makes good business sense. As we enter the new millennium, the average American employee works eighty-three hours a year more than his counterpart did in 1980. But, as has been alluded to, working longer hours does not necessarily mean a more productive organization. Louisa Wah, in an article in *Management Review*, states: "Recent estimates show that job stress costs employers over $200 billion a year in absenteeism, tardiness, lower productivity, and high turnover."[11] In a "work! work! work!" culture, the emotional health and well-being of employees also suffers. Jim Osterhaus of the Armstrong Group, a management consulting firm, comments: "If you don't attend to emotional health, instead of going up, your bottom line is going to go down." He cites the following disturbing statistics in organizations that do not foster emotional health:

- 18 percent of employees are not working to their full potential
- the average company spends 25 percent of after-tax profits on medical bills

- 15 percent of employees abuse alcohol and drugs
- morale tends to plummet, commitment decreases, turnover increases, productivity suffers, and profits decrease

Osterhaus continues, "In fact, the younger generation in the workforce expects companies to attend to their emotional balance as a matter of course. They are sophisticated about themselves; they aren't going to tolerate companies that use or abuse them. They're going to say, 'Nuts off, I'm going to go somewhere else.'"[12]

In a 1998 study commissioned by the Family and Work Institute (FWI), 3,351 U.S. workers demonstrated that being part of an organization that supports family is good for business. The study concluded that employees of a company deemed "supportive" of its employees demonstrated a high degree of job satisfaction. FWI president Ellen Galinsky noted that an employer's willingness to be flexible and responsive to the needs of employees is a powerful predictor of whether a worker would perform above and beyond normal expectations to provide added value to the company.[13] A Dupont study found that employees who took advantage of company based work-life programs were 45 percent more likely to "go the extra mile" for the organization. Similarly, NationsBank (now Bank of America) discovered that its turnover rate was reduced 50 percent among employees who used the company's work-family programs.[14] A recent study reported in the *Industrial Relations Journal* (which may, at first glance, seem contradictory) concluded that male employees who put family first made more money than those with other priorities. The study's coauthor, Jill Constantine of Williams College, explained that the results of the study are not that surprising. "What makes people desirable in the marriage market is also what makes them desirable in the job market. It has to do with how interested they are in making a relationship work."[15]

Many people erroneously assume that company work-life programs should be designed primarily for women who struggle to balance work and home. But the issue is fast becoming equally important to men. Companies who take into account both male and female employees will maximize their efforts to be family-friendly and will establish a gender-inclusive organizational culture. James Levine, a consultant and author of *Working Fathers*,[16] describes how men's values have changed over the years. He notes that "today's fathers want to have a different relationship with their kids than they did with their fathers. They grew up thinking something was missing and they want to change that." As a result, companies today are giving male employees the message that, as long as you get your job done, we will be flexible in allowing you to determine how and when you do it.[17]

A Harris Interactive poll for the Radcliffe Public Policy Center found that more than 80 percent of men between the ages of twenty and thirty-nine prefer a work schedule that allows for more time with family over a prestigious job. More than 70 percent of these men also said that they would be willing to give up a portion of their income in exchange for more time with their family. In contrast, only 26 percent of men surveyed over the age of sixty-five said they would trade pay for more family time. Similarly, 63 percent of younger women would give up pay for family time. Paula Rayman, a labor economist and director of the Radcliffe Center, told the *Washington Post*: "What we're seeing is a transformation between generations and gender. Young men are beginning to replicate women's sensibilities instead of women . . . trying to be more like men."[18]

Similarly, a 1999 PriceWaterhouseCoopers survey of twenty-five hundred college students from eleven countries found that 57 percent chose "attaining a balance between personal and career goals" as their number-one priority, compared to 45 percent of students in 1997. *Wall Street Journal* work and family expert Sue Shellenbarger reports that college recruits are beginning to ask more and more work-life balance questions of potential employers during interviews. She quotes Sandro Franchi, director of U.S. recruiting and staffing for Eli Lilly, who sums up the younger generation by stating, "Recruits want to know how do people work together, how are people treated, and is the work environment friendly and supportive."[19] Organizations that understand this generational and cultural shift also intuitively understand that providing a flexible, family-friendly, yet productive workplace is vital to their long-term success.

Creating a Family-Friendly Organizational Culture

The weight of this evidence forces the question upon today's Christian leaders: How can we create an office environment that encourages total commitment among employees, yet still enables them to balance professional and personal lives in a way that allows for meaning in both arenas? Some enlightened organizations today are attempting to achieve this balancing act by tailoring hours and expectations to employee needs, and are communicating a host of other messages: We will create work-life benefits and programs that will assist you in maintaining that healthy balance; we value your family life as much as we expect you to value your work responsibilities, and we will do everything in our power to help you balance these two competing roles; we know that there are times when work must necessarily come first; we are also aware that there are times when family must take precedence over the job; we are going to trust that you will be able to determine how your priorities will be ranked on any given day; we also trust that you will fulfill your role as an employee, and that you are aware of the consequences if you do not accomplish your objectives.

These programs will work only if they are implemented for the right reasons. If the goal is to get an employee to spend every waking moment working for the organization, the strategy will eventually fall apart. With few exceptions, today's employees are simply unwilling to sacrifice their lives for the good of the organization. They will quickly catch on to any plan they perceive to be manipulative. The implementation of such a plan may undermine their trust in the company, and they will quietly retaliate by lowering their productivity, becoming disloyal, and by leaving the organization.

Programs That Work

The task of creating a work-friendly organizational culture needs to be approached on three levels. First, the leadership team members must model a healthy work-life balance and demonstrate that they expect and encourage a similar balance in the lives of their subordinates. As discussed in the previous chapter, this requires the development of meaningful relationships between leaders and those they supervise. It will be a natural outcome of that relationship to ask questions that show a genuine interest in the members of the workforce: How is your family doing? How is your stress level? How can I help you accomplish your job responsibilities so that you do not continue to stay late at the office?

Second, the organization must look for ways to increase employee autonomy. The FWI has identified employee autonomy as a major factor in helping reduce turnover and increase employee loyalty.[20] Incentives aimed at developing autonomy, such as part-time telecommuting programs, flexible work schedules, and flexible-sick or personal-day programs, have been effective toward this end. My organization has given many of our senior managers home computers so they have the flexibility to work from home when the need arises. Those who take advantage of this option devote more total hours to the organization and are more productive than before, because they have a degree of freedom to choose when they will work. This arrangement has at the same time improved their work-life balance and overall morale.

Some companies allow time off as an incentive. Ohio-based Dawson Personnel Systems, a company that provides temporary workers, has experienced double-digit gains in sales largely as the result of a program that allows employees who meet elevated sales targets the freedom to leave work at 2:00 P.M. for the remainder of the month. Similarly, Aladdin Equipment, a Florida manufacturer of pool and spa replacement parts, switched its production schedule to nine-hour days, Monday through Thursday, with only a four-hour workday on Friday. This change helped Aladdin achieve a 50 percent reduction in absenteeism and a 10 percent increase in productivity.[21]

The best of the best employers are offering sabbaticals to help workers regain and maintain a life balance and to reconnect in a meaningful way to their families. The most comprehensive sabbatical program I have come across comes out of Arrow Electronics in Melville, New York. Arrow offers seven-year veterans of the company a ten-week paid sabbatical, which they may spend doing whatever they want. Between 1994 and 1999, more than fourteen hundred of its sixty-eight hundred North American employees took advantage of this opportunity.[22] I am writing this book during an eleven-week sabbatical that my organization has allowed me to take. The time has done wonders for my family and me. It has given me an opportunity to reassess my life, strengthen my relationship with God, reconnect with my family, view my organization's future from a new perspective, and return to work with renewed vigor. It has also provided our chief operating officer with the invaluable experience of serving as acting president—a key aspect of our board's transition plan for my eventual departure. Sabbaticals also serve as a great retention program for employees who are two or three years away from being vested. The retention savings from a well-run program offsets any increased costs from lost employee time.

Third, an organization that wants to create a family-friendly work environment has to develop a comprehensive benefits program aimed toward helping employees achieve balance in their lives. This may include providing a stellar health insurance program, access to a credit union, an employee exercise room, child care, employee counseling, and resources to help care for elderly parents. A *Time* magazine business report, "Perks That Work,"[23] noted that benefit options like telecommuting, on-site child care, parenting classes, referrals to elder care for aging parents, financial-planning services, long-term care insurance, job sharing, mental counseling services, and group auto and homeowners insurance had a positive influence on job retention and company loyalty.

From an employer perspective, the best practices dictate that an organization should blur the line between home and work whenever possible, thus easing the pressure many workers feel to be in two places at once. Kentucky-based Brown-Forman Corp., which produces Fetzer wines and Lenox china, provides employees with free on-site manicurists, hair stylists, shoe repair, personal trainers, and a vacation planner.[24] Other companies offer personal shoppers and in-house dry-cleaning services and stress management seminars. For a monthly fee, Circles.Com will help employees find a personal gift, make dinner reservations, get tickets for events or plays, and plan a vacation. J.C. Penney, at its Plano, Texas, headquarters, offers chef-prepared take-home meals. Texas Instruments provides its workers with child-rearing resources, rooms for nursing mothers to feed their babies, flexible scheduling, summer camps for children, a concierge to run errands, and an elder-care referral service. Ernst and Young likewise provides free concierge services to its fifteen hundred-plus consultants.[25]

What do organizations and their leaders get in return for such efforts and expense? Employees who are willing to work at home after hours and on weekends because they believe in the company's mission, feel they are able to make a difference, and appreciate the flexibility and trust that makes it possible for them to balance their lives. Galinsky comments that "employees with more supportive work-places are more willing than other workers to work harder than they have to in order to help their employers succeed."[26] Maxwell Locke & Ritter, an Austin-based accounting firm, found that intentional efforts to make its organizational culture more family-friendly resulted in decreased turnover and absenteeism, and improved productivity and employee morale.[27] Good employees will give back tenfold whatever it might cost the organization in expense to provide such flexibility. And the not-so-good employees? They will find an excuse not to work—flexible environment or not. But program benefits should not be formulated based on employees who perform poorly. This only makes mediocrity the standard and ultimately punishes higher-performing workers.

Biblical Advice

What insights about leading a balanced life can we gain from the Bible? Examples abound in the Scriptures, but one in particular stands out for me—a woman who "got it right." We read about her fully integrated life in Proverbs 31:10-31. Addington and Graves share with us:

> This woman got high marks from the customers in all the key sectors of her life. In the family area . . . her husband had full confidence in her (Prov. 31:11) and her children called her blessed (v. 28). Her business associates recognized that she was a wise investor (vv. 16 and 18), a conscientious employer (v. 15) and a hard worker (v. 17). In her community, she was known for caring for the poor (v. 20), and she was praised at the city gate for her "works" (v. 31).

Despite her many responsibilities, we don't get the sense that this woman is frustrated, overwhelmed, stressed out, or out of balance. Quite the opposite. Verse 25 says, "She is clothed with strength and dignity; she can laugh at the days to come. . . . [I]t's clear . . . that she had developed a reputation as a woman who feared the Lord. There was room in her busy life for God, and the results were obvious.[28]

The Bible also instructs us to live joyfully, without anxiety (Phil. 4:4-6); to be good stewards of our time, money, and talents (Matt. 25:14-30; Eph. 5:15, 16); to work with excellence (Col. 3:23); to attach ourselves to a community of believers (Heb. 10:25); and to raise our children in the training and instruction of the Lord (Eph. 6:4).[29] The Scriptures lay down sound principles for our personal and professional lives, but give us the freedom to make individual choices about how we apply those principles in order to improve ourselves and benefit our organization.

chapter seven

lead a life
of significance

*Aim at Heaven and you will get earth thrown in. Aim at earth and
you will get neither.*
—C. S. Lewis

When all is said and done, most
of us will have invested eighty thousand to one hundred thousand
hours of our lifetime in our profession. But to what purpose?
Chasing illusory success? Having the wrong career and slowly
dying—figuratively and literally—between weekends? Or living a
fulfilling life marked with purpose and passion? God did not
intend that we should merely endure our work. Rather, God
intended that we engage work as a gift and vocation, as a profound opportunity to participate—in what we do for a living and
in God's creation. Work is meant to give meaning to our lives,
improve the world in which we live, and provide a daily opportunity for us to be witnesses for Christ.

The Golden Rule of Leadership is not a new concept. It is an
old concept, at least as old as the Christian tradition, and business
leaders have tried to apply it to business practice before. In seven-
teenth-century England, for example, *caveat emptor* was the order
of the day, cautioning buyers against untrustworthy merchants.
In that same century, George Fox, founder of the Society of
Friends (Quakers), encouraged a new business ethic based on

truthfulness, dependability, and fixed prices. For Fox, this was the only logical outcome of practicing one's faith in the world of business. Quaker businessmen heeded his call, quickly became perceived as some of the few people who could be trusted, and became extremely successful.[1] Their success forced other businessmen to adopt the Quaker ethical model in order to survive in the marketplace. Imagine the radical leap of faith these Quakers initially had to take in order to bring about such significant changes in the business world.

Fast forward to the United States, and one finds similar examples. J.C. Penney, founder of the department store chain, which included 175 stores by 1917, believed wholeheartedly in the value of biblically based leadership. He even referred to the Bible as "a pretty fine business textbook!" Penney commented on how just one of the Bible's principles applies to business:

> I refer to the declaration that if a man would be first among you, let him become your servant. That principle is at the foundation of business success. I think it would be a good idea if the business colleges would include the Bible in their list of textbooks. I suppose its value lies in the fact that it teaches character, which is the very fundamental of success.[2]

More recently, Collins and Porras show how truly visionary companies, such as 3M, American Express, Boeing, General Electric, Johnson & Johnson, and Hewlett Packard, understand the importance of creating and sustaining an organizational vision and a core set of values that have integrity and stand the test of time. Their empirical data demonstrate how organizations that successfully articulate their core values and align their actions accordingly will, over the long term, significantly increase their value.

Following the Golden Rule of Leadership not only has a favorable impact on organizations, but on our personal lives as well. Thomas Stanley, in *The Millionaire's Mind*,[3] describes how the financial success of the wealthy can be attributed largely to traits they have in common. He found that being well disciplined, honest, focused, willing to take chances, and having a love for what one does are much more important than IQ or the caliber of business school attended. These same qualities are demonstrated also in people whose success cannot be accounted by mere dollars. They can also be seen, for example, in a Houston area couple, Mark and Susan Long. As foster parents, the Longs have for fifteen years cared for more than fifty medically fragile children including Emily, a two-year-old paraplegic, and three-year-old Billy, who, as the result of being severely beaten, is blind and can barely swallow. Having combined "millionaire traits" with the golden rule, the Longs are leading a life of significance. When the Golden Rule of Leadership is entwined with a passionate and purposeful career, the result is a marriage that reaps spiritual and earthly blessings.

Being a business leader and a Christian does not guarantee automatic success to an organization. Christian or not, an organization and its leaders can go adrift. A leader may, for example, be at a point in his or her career in which the feeling of being called to leadership is absent. A leader's life may lack balance, causing organizational disarray. Corrective action in any of these circumstances may, for some, be merely a matter of sharpening focus. For others, it may mean pursuing a new career. Leadership, like life, is not a destination but a journey.

Three Modes of Leadership

In my study of leaders from the executive suite to the parish, and positions in between, I have concluded that every leader operates within one of three modes of leadership: survival, success, or significance. Leaders who are in the survival mode are struggling to keep the doors of their organization open. It is likely that such leaders themselves are living lives that are out of balance. They are fighting a losing battle with changing market forces, clinging to outmoded or ineffective leadership styles, or generally failing to follow the Golden Rule of Leadership. Their talents and passions are not aligned with their current position. These individuals are often inattentive, lack commitment to their work, and produce haphazard results. This category of leader includes those who have essentially retired on the job, counting the days to their retirement or their departure. The fire inside has died and they are living out their days hoping no crises or opportunities arise while they remain on watch.

The second mode of leadership is characterized by the idea of success. A success mode leader has attained financial success, power, and notoriety, but senses that something is still missing. Her external display of happiness is shallow and insincere, and it often masks personal angst and fear. This leader may well be terrified at the thought of death or the idea of being alone, and may be on a constant quest for the "fountain of youth" or the latest toy. This leader may use those around him or her as tools to achieve personal goals. Leaders operating in this mode have truly lost any sense of balance—and a connectedness to their faith—and leave behind them lives littered with incidents of alcoholism, depression, troubled children, divorce, and estranged relationships. For them, meaning is connected to their position in life and the size of their bank account. They are living proof of the irony that those who strive for success as an end in itself will never achieve it.

The notion of significance describes the third mode of leadership. A leader in this mode has discovered his gifts and passion and combines the two through work and family to bring meaning to individual and community life. This leader uses his position to add true value to the world and to the lives of others. He truly understands the Golden Rule of Leadership and the importance of balancing faith, life, and work. A leader of significance has come to know that God's gift of life matters, and that human beings are instruments of God's bidding—that God has "equipped us for His purposes" (1 Cor. 12:4-7). When one operates in the significance mode of leadership, genuine satisfaction and joy follow as true servant leadership is practiced. In the words of Leo Tolstoy, a significance-mode leader understands that "Life is a place of service. Joy can be real only if people look upon their life as service."

One does not attain this level of leadership by building a business empire or by garnering impressive titles. Significance is derived from the impact we have on those around us. Let me share with you a story told to me by Albert Siu, former chief learning officer for AT&T. Albert was visiting one of the famous Bell Labs, where researchers were using light instead of electricity to transmit information. Because elements such as light or sound dissipate over distance, they were struggling with how to sustain the intensity of light. Posted on the lab wall was a chart of atoms. During his visit, Albert learned that there were more than fifty types of atoms, to which Bell scientists had assigned pet names. They were listed in rank-order, so that atom number 1 is the "big shot" and number 51 is lowest on the totem pole. At number 49 was an atom they had named Kirby. When they directed a laser through Kirby, the atom, instead of blocking the light, magnified it! Albert's point was that it is not the atom's size or rank-order that was important. Even small and lowly Kirby has tremendous value and purpose. When enough Kirbys are placed at the right intervals, light can have an infinite reach.

In the midst of tackling the challenges of our day-to-day lives, we may, at times, feel a little like Kirby—small and insignif-icant. But if we step back and see that we are connected to a net-work of other committed people, we will become energized and inspired. What matters is not our position or rank in life—multi-billion-dollar enterprise or Mom and Pop corner store, famous or unknown, CEO or housekeeper. What matters is trusting that wherever we are, we reflect the infinite light of God's grace and hope to those around us.

Magnifying Our Faith

No matter what it is we do for a living—sales, software, academia, parish, manufacturing, social services, distribution—we are essentially all in the same business: magnifying our Christian faith by serving others. It is a useful exercise to give oneself an honest performance review by asking, "Who am I serving?" From time to time, we all need to reflect on what mode of leadership we are currently functioning within. Embarking on a lifestyle of daily service to others will elevate our leadership mode from survival or success to significance. And we must always keep in mind that while there are many ways to serve, at the end of the day we all serve the same Lord.

At times, we may become acutely aware that we are in the wrong career position. Despite our best efforts, we are not adding value to those around us and are not leading a life of significance. At such times, there is no need to be discouraged. We have all been there. For me, it was during my time as a civil litigation attorney. My leadership mode during that time fell somewhere between survival and success. I simply did not feel fulfilled working in a career where my sole purpose was to transfer large amounts of money from one corporation to another. Even Peter Drucker has been there. He quit his lucrative job as an investment banker in the mid-1930s—in the middle of the Great Depression and without another job prospect—because he did not feel that he was making a true contribution. Drucker made this decision to leave because, in his words, "People, I realized, were what I valued, and I saw no point in being the richest man in the cemetery." He continues, "Values . . . are and should be the ultimate test."[4]

As Drucker and so many others have proven, being in a job where you feel temporarily "out of alignment" is not a life sentence. We are fortunate to be living in a time when it is possible to pursue several careers in one lifetime; we can take one step back to move two steps forward. In fact, sometimes our Lord uses the "unaligned" periods in our life to prepare us for positions of significance later in life. The prophet Jeremiah pronounces what plans God has for us—and we can draw some comfort that there is more than one plan. Greg Bourgond describes it this way:

> The good news is that God is not finished with us yet. He is a God of second, third, and fourth chances. The roads we choose in any given instance simply provide a new set of opportunities to live a legacy worth leaving. We may suffer some consequences, but we shouldn't be discouraged. God is merciful and full of grace.[5]

Some of us have found our purpose in life, and some of us are still searching. Earlier, I recommended Richard Leider's *Power of Purpose: Creating Meaning in Your Life and Work*,[6] which has been of great help to me. Leider defines one's calling as "the inner urge to give your gifts away." He says each of us is uniquely gifted and each has a purpose in life. The key is for us to discover our gifts, unwrap what we have been given, and give our gifts away. As Aristotle once said, "Where your talents and the needs of the world cross, therein lies your calling, your vocation." Failure to respond to our calling in life will slowly kill us from the inside out, Leider warns. You know when you have answered the call, says Leider, when you are "living in the place you belong with the people you love doing the right work on purpose."

People who are facing death often have a better handle than do "healthy" individuals on what living a life of significance really means. Elisabeth Kübler-Ross suggests three questions for the dying to ask of themselves, all of which place a premium on significance: "Did I give and receive love?" "Did I become all I can be?" "Did I leave the world a better place?"[7] When all is said and done, we human beings have a deep desire to leave a legacy, to leave a part of ourselves with the world after we die. The legacy we leave will be defined by how we have reared our children, by how we have followed our passion, by the influence we have had on those around us, and by the resources we have left to support the causes we believe in. The legacy we leave as a leader will be similarly defined, and answering Kübler-Ross's questions from time to time is a good way to track its development.

Being a true leader is difficult and takes a huge commitment and sacrifice. Jesus does not mince words on the subject of such responsibility: "From everyone who has been given much, much will be demanded; and from the one who has been entrusted with much, much more will be asked" (Luke 12:48). Being a servant leader, building a healthy organizational culture, creating and implementing an effective strategic plan, mentoring those around us, and staying meaningfully connected to family are all aspects of a full-time calling. However, if we live as children of God and stay true to our calling, the rewards will be great. Life will have purpose, we will know true joy, and we will create value in an organization and its people that will continue to have an impact long after we are gone. In short, we will be leading lives of significance. I have worked in nonprofit and for-profit settings, colleges and human-care organizations, for politicians and law firms, for lots of money and for very little money, and I have found that the only true fulfillment in life comes from building a better world.

What kind of influence can you and I have? Probably more than you think. A single story, when told on *60 Minutes* or reported in the *Wall Street Journal,* can affect the fortunes of entire organizations. Imagine the difference fifty million Christians can make—people who strive to make ourselves, our organizations, and our world a better place. This influence occurs through our roles as sales clerks, certified nursing assistants, accountants, investment advisors, pastors, politicians, organizational leaders, and CEOs, as each of us works at following the Golden Rule of Leadership and convincing others of its value.

From the Bible, we learn that God considers our efforts in the workplace to improve the world very important. In the Old Testament, God refers to a craftsman named Bezalel as being "filled with my Spirit to work in gold and silver."[8] And while we remember the apostle Paul as a great missionary, a great communicator, and a great servant-leader, it was his skill as a tentmaker that paid the bills. Each of us has been chosen and equipped to honor God through our daily work. As a product of God's handiwork, we need to be true to the golden rule by doing unto others what we would have them do to us. We thereby discover our passion and purpose in life. We discover that true leadership is a blessing to be shared with all.

I remember as a child listening to the story of Jesus' healing of the ten lepers, and of how only one returned to thank him. I thought to myself at the time, "There's no way I would be like the other nine and not return to offer my thanks." Of course, I have not always lived up to my youthful ideal. We all forget, at times, to thank our Lord for his many blessings, not the least of which is the ability to lead. God has given us vision; equipped us with tools and experience to face daily challenges and add value to God's kingdom; empowered us with wisdom to make the right decisions; and rewarded us for faithfully following God's Word and serving as God's humble servant.[9]

Business magazines and books today talk about success as a product of building a brand or managing a company of one. A servant-leader looks at it from a different perspective: We will be successful, whatever we do and wherever we go, if we faithfully follow the Golden Rule of Leadership, and live our life for an audience of one—Jesus Christ. Through our everyday actions in life, we are, in effect, walking advertisements for our faithful God.

notes

Introduction: Doing Well by Doing Good
1. Nashville: Thomas Nelson, 1994.

Chapter 1: Follow the Golden Rule of Leadership
1. Quoted Andrew Fineman, "A Call to Authenticity," *The Life@Work Journal,* (March–April 2000), 20.
2. Brad Hewitt, interview with author, 19 April 2001.
3. Some of the ideas for this paragraph came from Perry Pascarella, *Christ Centered Leadership: Thriving in Business by Putting God in Charge* (Rockland, Calif.: Prima Publishing, 1999).
4. Ken Blanchard, Bill Hybels, and Phil Hodges, *Leadership by the Book: Tools to Transform Your Workplace* (New York: Waterbook Press, 1999).
5. Richard Leider, *The Power of Purpose: Creating Meaning in Your Life and Work* (San Francisco: Berrett-Koehler, 1997).
6. Kevin Cashman, *Leadership from the Inside Out: Becoming a Leader for Life* (Provo: Executive Excellence Publishing, 1999).
7. Gene Wilkes, *Jesus on Leadership* (Wheaton, Ill.: Tyndale House, 1998).
8. Blanchard, Hybels, and Hodges.
9. Blanchard, Hybels, and Hodges, 53.
10. Robert Greenleaf, *Servant Leadership: A Journey into the Nature of Legitimate Power and Greatness* (New York: Paulist Press, 1991).
11. Laurie Beth Jones, *Jesus, CEO: Using Ancient Wisdom for Visionary Leadership* (New York: Hyperion, 1995).
12. Max DePree, *Leadership Is an Art* (New York: Doubleday, 1989).
13. Max DePree, *Leadership Jazz* (New York, Doubleday, 1992).
14. James C. Hunter, *The Servant: A Simple Story about the True Essence of Leadership* (Roseville, Calif.: Prima Publishing, 1998).
15. Bobby Griffin, telephone interview with author, 21 June 2001.
16. Quoted in Michael Barrier, "Leadership Skills Employees Respect," *Nation's Business* (January 1999), 28, 30.
17. F. F. Richheld, *The Loyalty Effect: The Hidden Force Behind Growth, Profits, and Lasting Value* (Boston: Harvard Business School Press, 1996), quoted in Robert Banks, "Moving from Faith to Faithfulness," in *Faith in Leadership: How Leaders Live Out*

Their Faith in Their Work and Why It Matters, edited by Robert Banks and Kimberly Powell. (San Francisco: Jossey Bass, 2000), 17.

18. Francis Fukuyama, *The Social Virtues and the Creation of Prosperity* (New York: Free Press, 1995), quoted in Carlton J. Snow, "Building Trust in the Fractured Workplace," in *Faith in Leadership*, 36.

19. Harold Burson, "Letters to the Editor," *Wall Street Journal*, 22 January 1999, sec. A, 11.

20. Quoted in J. P. Donlon, "Guess Who's the Chief Reputation Officer?" *Chief Executive* (March 2001), 44–46.

21. Ibid., 46.

22. Quoted in Jim Barlow, "Improve the Firm; Listen to Workers," *Houston Chronicle*, 8 December 1998, sec. C, 1.

23. Quoted in Thomas J. Neff, James M. Citron, and Spencer Stewart, "Doing the Right Things Right," *Chief Executive* (February 2000), 54, 56.

24. *Fast Company*, March 2001, 124.

25. Ronald A. Heifetz, *Leadership without Easy Answers* (Cambridge, Mass.: Belnap Press, 1994).

26. Ronald A. Heifetz and Donald Laurie, "The Work of Leadership," *Harvard Business Review* (January–February 1997), 124–25.

27. Heifetz, *Leadership without Easy Answers*, 3.

28. U.S. House Majority Leader Tom DeLay, interview with author, 16 August 2001.

29. Richard Higginson, "Integrity and the Art of Compromise," in *Faith in Leadership*, 31–32.

Chapter 2: Create an Effective Organizational Culture

1. Quoted in Jeanne Dugan Ianthe, "The Siren Song of the Silicon Valley," *Washington Post*, 17 April 2000, Weekly Edition, 18.

2. Ibid.

3. "Doing Well by Doing Good: Building Communities and the Bottom Line," an Address by Jeffrey B. Swartz, president and CEO, The Timberland Company, 24 October 2000, Independent Sector Annual Conference: www.independentsector.org.

4. Sue Shellenbarger, "To Win the Loyalty of Your Employees, Try a Softer Touch," *Wall Street Journal*, 26 January 2000, sec. B, 1.

5. George Donnelly, "Recruiting, Retention and Returns," *CFO* (March 2001), 68, 70.

6. Quoted in Gary Hamel, "Reinvent Your Company," *Fortune* (12 June 2000), 103.

7. Comment made at Lutheran Brotherhood Board Meeting, 8 March 2001.

8. Tom Peters, "Leadership Is Confusing As Hell," *Fast Company* (March 2001), 124, 138.

9. James C. Collins and Jerry I. Porras, *Built to Last: Successful Habits of Visionary Companies* (New York: Harper Business, 1994), 46.

10. Kevin Maney, "Failure to Define Company's Purpose Led to AT&T's 4-Way Split," *USA Today*, 1 November 2000, sec. B, 3.

11. Jeffrey Ball and Scott Miller, "DaimlerChrysler Director Claims U.S. Executives Withheld Data," *Wall Street Journal*, 4 December 2000, sec. A, 4.

12. David S. Pottruck, "New World, Old Traditions," *Chief Executive* (November 2000), 36–40.

13. "Commitment Pays," *Wall Street Journal*, 11 January 2000, sec. A, 1.

14. Lutheran Brotherhood and Aid Association for Lutherans merged on January 1, 2002, and became Thrivent Financial For Lutherans.

15. Beth Fratzke, "True Confessions of an LB Employee," *Life* (September–October 2000), 18. *Life* is an internal publication for Lutheran Brotherhood employees.

16. See, for example, Clint Carpenter, "For-Profits Polish Image with Volunteering," *The Non-Profit Times* (March 2000), 4; Rodney Ho, Rebecca Smith, and Jim Carlton, "Some Firms Tout Benefits of a Social Conscience," *Wall Street Journal*, 3 December 1999, sec. A, 6.

17. Personal interview with author, 19 April 2001.

18. Richard Boulton, Barry Libert, and Steve Samek, *Cracking the Value Code: How Successful Businesses Are Creating Wealth in the New Economy* (New York: Harper Collins, 2000), 17–19.

19. Rachel Emma Silverman, "The Jungle: What's News in Recruitment and Pay," *Wall Street Journal*, 29 August 2000, sec. B, 14.

20. Kris Frieswick, "Employee Retention: A Costly Revolving Door," *CFO* (October 2000), 28.

21. Boulton et al, 37–38.

22. Diana Kunde, "Tight Market Forces Employers to Devise Ways to Keep Top Talent," *Dallas Morning News*, 11 November 1998, sec. D, 1.

23. Howard Schultz, "The Management Course for Presidents," *Best Practices Case Study: Managing Culture* (New York: American Management Association), 1.

24. Donnelly, 68.

25. Bob Woods, "The Challenges for Leaders in the New Economy: An interview with James E. Copeland, Jr." *Chief Executive* (August 2000), 3, 5.

26. Quoted in Rebecca Buckkman, "Keeping on Course in a Crisis," *Wall Street Journal*, 9 June 2000, sec. B, 1.

27. Marcus Buckingham and Curt Coffman, *First Break All the Rules: What the World's Greatest Managers Do Differently* (New York: Simon and Schuster, 1999), 33.

28. Donnelly, 74.

29. Laura D'Andrea Tyson, "After Irrational Exuberance, Irrational Pessimism," *Business Week* (12 August 2002), 22.

30. Mark Williams, "Prophet Sharing with Peter Drucker," Redherring.com, 26 January 2001.

31. Ibid.

32. Joan Urdang, "Money Isn't Everything," *CFO* (March 2001), 16.

33. Scott Thuran, "How to Drive an Express Train," *Wall Street Journal*, 6 June 2000, sec. B, 1, 4.

34. Personal interview with author, 3 July 2001. For a more detailed description of how one professional services firm implemented their version of the golden rule, see Earl Maxwell, *Service, Prosperity, and Sanity: Positioning the Professional Service Firm for the Future* (Austin: Maxwell, Locke, & Ritter, 1998).

35. Sue Schellenbarger, "An Overlooked Toll of Job Upheavals: Valuable Friendships," *Wall Street Journal*, 12 January 2000, sec. B, 1.

36. Peter Cappelli, "A Market-Driven Approach to Retaining Talent," *Harvard Business Review* (January–February 2000).

37. Oren Harari, "The Road Runner Millenium," *Management Review* (January 2000), 29, 31.

38. Angela Shah, "Employers Find a Benefit in Providing for Workers," *Dallas Morning News*, 27 July 2000, sec. D, 1.

39. Pui-Wing Tam, "Silicon Valley Belatedly Boots Up Programs to Ease Employees' Lives," *Wall Street Journal*, 29 August 2000, sec. B, 1.

40. Paula Schlueter Ross, "Angels in the Workplace," *The Lutheran Witness* (October 2000), 6–7.

41. Marilyn Chase, "Healthy Assets: Corporations Are Discovering That it Can Pay to Keep Their Employees Fit," *Wall Street Journal*, 1 May 2000, sec. R, 9.

42. Barry Lynn, "Going Green in Shades of Gray," *American Way* (15 March 2001), 102, 105.

Chapter 3: Do the Right Thing

1. Stephen L. Carter, *Integrity* (New York: Basic Books, 1996), 6, quoted in, Perry Pascurella, *Christ Centered Leadership: Thriving in Business by Putting God in Charge* (Rocklin, Calif.: Prima Publishing, 1999), 103.

2. Maria Mallory, "Liar, Liar, Workplace Ire," *Austin American-Statesman*, 3 September 2000, sec. K, 1.

3. New York: Harper Business, 1994

4. "Value Creation: The 'Either/Or Question,'" *Management Review* (November 1998), 7.

5. Stephen Barr, "Guilty As Charged," *CFO* (April 1999), 28.

6. Milo Geyelin, "How an Internal Memo Written 26 Years Ago Is Costing GM Dearly," *Wall Street Journal*, 29 September 1999, sec. A, 1.

7. Gregory L. White and Karen Lundegaard, "Ford Says Last Year's Quality Snafus Took Big Toll—Over $1 Billion in Profit," *Wall Street Journal*, 12 January 2001, sec. A, 3.

8. Marianne M. Jennings, "Ford-Firestone Lesson: Heed the Moment of Truth," *Wall Street Journal*, 11 September 2000, sec. A, 44.

9. Brock Yates, "Why Couldn't This Marriage Be Saved," *Wall Street Journal*, 29 May 2001, sec. A, 22.

10. Jennings, sec. A, 44.

11. James C. Collins and Jerry I. Porras, *Built to Last: Successful Habits of Visionary Companies* (New York: Harper Business, 1994), 58.

12. The full text of Johnson & Johnson's "Our Credo" (in several dozen languages) and a history of its development can be seen at the company's Web site (www.jnj.com).

13. *Built to Last*, 61.

14. Richard Boulton, Barry Libert, and Steve Samek, *Cracking the Value Code: How Successful Businesses Are Creating Wealth in the New Economy* (New York: Harper Business, 2000), 114.

15. "New Ford Boss Is Different, on Purpose," *St. Louis Post-Dispatch*, 1 January 1999, sec. C, 1.

16. Patrick Barta, "In Current Expansion, As Business Booms, So, Too, Do Layoffs," *Wall Street Journal*, 13 March 2000, sec. A, 1.

17. Jon E. Hilsenrath, "Many Say Layoffs Hurt Companies More Than They Help," *Wall Street Journal*, 21 February 2001, sec. A, 2.

18. Ibid.

19. "You Can Quote Him," *Fast Company* (July 2001), 66, 68.

20. Kemba J. Dunham, "The Kinder, Gentler Way to Lay Off Employees," *Wall Street Journal*, 13 March 2001, sec. B, 1.

21. Ibid., 48.

22. *Built to Last*, 60.

23. Don Bokenkamp, telephone interview with author, 6 July 2001.

24. Jeremy Rifkin, *The Age of Access* (New York: Putnam, 2000), 48.

25. Rodney Ho, Rebecca Smith, and Jim Carlton, "Some Firms Tout Benefits of a Social Conscience," *Wall Street Journal*, 3 December 1999, sec. A, 6.

26. Barry Lynn, "Going Green in Shades of Gray," *American Way* (15 March 2001), 102, 105–111.

27. Gene Koretz, "On Wall Street, Green Is Golden: Eco Concern Is Paying Dividends," *Business Week* (8 January 2001).

28. Lorraine Monroe, "Leadership Is about Making a Vision Happen—What I Call 'Vision Acts,'" *Fast Company* (March 2001), 98.

29. John Mackovic, telephone interview with author, 3 July 2001.

30. Presentation to the Lutheran Brotherhood Board of Directors, 25 January 2001.

31. Rebecca Blumenstein, "AT&T Now Is Facing Erosion in Key Sector: Its Business Customers," *Wall Street Journal*, 11 August 2000, sec. A, 1, 6.

32. Andrew Park, "Experience Weighs on Netpliance," *Austin American-Statesman*, 16 April 2001, sec. E, 3.

33. *Built to Last*, 1.

34. Richard J. Leider, *The Power of Purpose: Creating Meaning in Your Life and Work* (San Francisco: Berrett-Koehler, 1997), 20–21.

35. Richard Kessler, telephone interview with author, 20 June 2001.

Chapter 4: Values-Based Strategic Planning

1. Ken Blanchard, Bill Hybels, and Phil Hodges, *Leadership by the Book: Tools to Transform Your Workplace* (New York: Waterbrook Press, 1999), 173.

2. Richard T. Pascale, Mark Millemann, and Linda Gioja, *Surfing the Edge of Chaos: The Laws of Nature and the New Laws of Business* (New York: Crown Business, 2000).

3. Lynn Walker, telephone interview with author, 2 July 2001.

4. Mark Albion, *Making a Life, Making a Living* (New York: Warner Business Books, 2000), 100.

5. Many of the ideas from the proceeding paragraph were obtained from *Executive Resource* (Fall 1996), published by Kipp & Associates, Nashville.

6. Andrea Gabor, "Creating a New Corporation: "How Peter Drucker Radically Changed American Business," *U.S. News & World Report* (8 May 2000), 42.

7. "Rethinking Strategy/Part 2: An Interview with Dr. Gary Hamel," *Leadership* (December 1998), 2–3. *Leadership* is a publication of the American Management Association.

8. Quoted in Sheila Wellington, "Succeeding in Adversity Makes Success All the Sweeter," *Fast Company* (May 2001), 84.

9. John P. Kotter, *Leading Change* (Cambridge, Mass.: Harvard Business School Press, 1996), 90.

10. Regina Fazio Maruca, ed., "Masters of Disaster," *Fast Company* (April 2001), 92.

11. Ibid.

12. Gerald F. Davis and Michael Useem, "Governance Leadership and Convergence," *The Corporate Board* (March–April 2001), 17.

13. Robert A. Watson & Ben Brown (New York: Crown Business, 2001).

14. New York: HarperCollins, 2001.

15. James C. Collins and Jerry Porras, *Built to Last: Successful Habits of Visionary Companies* (New York: Harper Business, 1994), 201–202. Emphasis theirs.

16. Ibid., 211–16.

17. Ibid., 94.

18. Ibid., 105. Emphasis theirs.

19. (Cambridge: Harvard Business School Press, 1996), 3–16.

20. Ibid., 33–158.

21. Ibid., 35.

22. (New York: McGraw Hill, 1997), 17.

23. Ibid.

24. Bob Woods, "The Challenges for Leaders in the New Economy: An interview with James E. Copeland, Jr.," *Chief Executive Guide* (August 2000), 3, 4.

Chapter 5: Develop and Mentor a Leadership Team

1. Glen Kehrein, "The Local Church and Christian Community Development," in *Restoring At-Risk Communities: Doing It Together & Doing It Right,* John Perkins, ed., (Grand Rapids: Baker Books, 1995), 163, 184–86.

2. Quoted from Richard J. Leider, *The Power of Purpose: Creating Meaning in Your Life and Work* (San Francisco: Berrett-Koehler, 1997), 139.

3. Ken Blanchard, Bill Hybels, and Phil Hodges, *Leadership by the Book: Tools to Transform Your Workplace* (New York: Waterbrook Press,1999), 66–67.

4. Noel M. Tichy with Eli Cohen, *The Leadership Engine: How Winning Companies Build Leaders at Every Level* (New York: HarperBusiness, 1997).

5. Quoted in Carol Kleiman, "Flexibility at Workplace Not a Stretch," *Austin American-Statesman,* 7 May 2000, sec. F, 1.

6. Carlos Tejada, "Disengaged at Work? Such Workers Cost Billions, a Study Concludes," *Wall Street Journal,* 13 March 2001, sec. A, 1.

7. Thomas O. Davenport, "Human Capital: Employees Want a Return on Their Investment and Expect Managers to Help Them Get It," *Management Review* (December 1999), 37, 40.

8. "An Ounce of Prevention," *Management Review* (October 1998), 9.

9. Davenport, 39.

10. Ibid., 38.

11. Quoted in, "Built for Speed," *Chief Executive* (October 2000), 58, 64.

12. "15 Ways to Greater Employee Retention," *American Management Association's Mworld* (10 July 2000), www.amanet.org.

13. Carol Hymowitz, "How to Tell Employees All the Things They Don't Want to Hear," *The Wall Street Journal,* 22 August 2000, sec. B, 1.

14. Michael J. McDermott, "New Policies for MetLife Managers," *Chief Executive Guide* (August 2000), 29.

15. Carol Hymowitz, "Readers Tell Tales of Success and Failure Using Rating Systems," *Wall Street Journal,* 29 May 2001, sec. B, 1.

16. Lynn Walker, telephone interview with author, 2 July 2001.

17. The details of implementing such a plan are beyond the scope of this chapter. For those who would like additional information, a good resource to start with is, Robert S. Kaplan and David P. Norton, "Using the Balanced Scorecard As a Strategic Management System, *Harvard Business Review* (January–February 1996).

18. "Growing the Next Generation: Mentoring Is a Tool for Cultivating New Leaders," *Life@Work Journal* (September 1998), 18, 20.

19. Ibid., 20–21.

20. Jim Hushagen, telephone interview with author, 13 August 2001.

21. W. Chan Kim and Renee Mauborgne, "Fair Process: Managing in the Knowledge Economy," *Harvard Business Review,* July–August 1997, 66.

22. Some of the ideas in this paragraph were the result of reading James C. Hunter, *The Servant: A Simple Story about the True Essence of Leadership* (Roseville, Calif.: Prima Publishing, 1998), 91–125.

23. The "one-anothers," *The Life@Work Journal* (March–April 2000), 48.

Chapter 6: Balancing Family and Professional Life

1. Kirstin Downey Grimsley, "No Time? No Problem: Many Companies Are Offering Creative Perks to Help Stressed-Out Employees," *Washington Post*, 13 March 2000. Weekly Edition, sec. P, 8.
2. Robert Reich, *The Future of Success* (New York: Alfred A. Knopf, 2001), 118–19.
3. Grimsley, 8.
4. Michael Hickins, "Give a Little, Get a Lot," *Management Review* (October 1998), 6.
5. *Executive Health*, Lutheran Church–Missouri Synod Health Ministries and Department of Human Resources, February 2001.
6. Arlie Russell Hochschild, *The Time Bind: When Work Becomes Home and Home Becomes Work* (New York: Henry Holt and Co., 1997), as quoted in Dennis Rainey, "Is Work Home?" *Life@Work* (May–June 2000), 10.
7. Dale Dauten, "Help at the Office Hard to Come By," *Chicago Tribune*, 29 October 2000, sec. 5, 8.
8. July–August 1999.
9. *The Age Of Access* (New York: Tarcher/Putnam, 2000).
10. New York: Simon & Schuster, 1994.
11. Louisa Wah, "The Emotional Tightrope," *Management Review* (January 2000), 38.
12. Ibid., 39.
13. "Work/Life Balance: Give a Little, Get a Lot," *Management Review* (October 1998), 6.
14. Ibid.
15. "InBox," *Life@Work Journal* (March–April 2000), 19.
16. James Levine, *Working Fathers: New Strategies for Balancing Work and Family* (New York: Harcourt, Brace & Co., 1997).
17. Quoted in, Gayle Vassar Melvin, "Fathers Working for Family Life," *Austin American-Statesman*, 20 November 1998, sec. F, 6.
18. Kristin Downey Grimsley, "Making Family a Priority: Young Men Say a Flexible Work Schedule Is More Important Than a High Salary," *Washington Post*, 8 May 2000, National Weekly Edition, 34.
19. Sue Shellenbarger, "What Job Candidates Really Want to Know: Will I Have a Life?" *Wall Street Journal*, 17 November 1999, sec. B, 1.
20. Thomas O. Davenport, "Human Capital: Employees Want a return on Their Investment and They Expect Managers to Help Them Get It," *Management Review* (December 1999), 37, 41.
21. Sue Shellenbarger, "For Harried Workers in the 21st Century, Six Trends to Watch," *Wall Street Journal*, 29 December 1999, sec. B, 1.
22. Louisa Wah, "The Emotional Tightrope," *Management Review* (January 2000), 38, 40.
23. Laura Koss-Feder, "Perks That Work," *Time, Time Select Business Report* (9 November 1998).
24. "Work Week: A Special News Report about Life on the Job—and Trends Taking Shape There," *Wall Street Journal*, 22 December 1998, sec. A, 1.
25. Kirstin Downey Grimsley, "No Time? No Problem: Many Companies Are Offering Creative Perks to Help Stressed-Out Employees," *Washington Post*, 13 March 2000, Weekly Edition, 8.
26. Michael Hickins, "Give a Little, Get a Lot," *Management Review* (October 1998), 6.
27. Earl Maxwell, *Service, Prosperity and Sanity: Positioning the Professional Service Firm for the Future* (Austin: Maxwell Locke & Ritter, 1998), 132.
28. Thomas Addington and Thomas Graves, "Balance: Life's Juggling Act, *Life@Work* (November–December 2000), 40, 43.
29. Ibid., 47.

Chapter 7: Lead a Life of Significance

1. Robert K. Greenleaf, *Servant Leadership: A Journey into the Nature of Legitimate Power and Greatness* (New York: Paulist Press, 1977), 143.
2. J. C. Penney, "It Is One Thing to Desire—And Another to Determine," in *The Book of Business Wisdom: Classic Writings by the Legends of Commerce and Industry*, Peter Krass, ed. (New York: John Wiley and Sons, 1997), 85, 89.
3. Thomas Stanley, *The Millionaire's Mind* (New York: Andrews McMeel, 2000).
4. Peter Drucker, "Managing Oneself," *Harvard Business Review* (March–April 1999), 65, 70.
5. Greg Bourgond, "The Significance Factor: Keys to Leaving a Godly Legacy," *Life @ Work* (January–February 2000), 69, 71.
6. Richard Leider, *Power of Purpose: Creating Meaning in Your Life and Work* (San Francisco: Berrett-Koehler, 1997).
7. Quoted in Richard J. Leider and David A. Shapiro, *Whistle While You Work: Heeding Your Life's Calling* (San Francisco: Berrett-Koehler, 2001), 140.
8. See Exodus 35:30–33.
9. Some of these thoughts were inspired by reading Bill Hybels, "The Wonder of It All: Unwrapping the Gift of Leadership," *Life @ Work* (September–October 2000), 58.